AN OLD TESTAMENT DEVOTIONAL SERIES

WALKING IN THE WAY

A Devotional Journey Through the Scriptures Jesus Read

TOBY SHOCKEY

DEDICATION

To Hannah,

Psalms 37:23-24 says, "The steps of a man are established by the LORD, when he delights in his way; though he fall, he shall not be cast headlong, for the LORD upholds his hand." If your dad has a single favorite passage of Scripture, this may be the one. I won't be able to be there with you in everything you will face in your life, but I can point you to the Scriptures and to the specific passages that God used to guide and encourage me along the way. May you sense His presence, follow His path at every turn and know His gracious hand to pick you up when you fall.

And here is one more:

"The salvation of the righteous is from the LORD; he is their stronghold in the time of trouble. The LORD helps them and delivers them; he delivers them from the wicked and saves them, because they take refuge in him." Psalms 37:39-40

Love,
Dad

Walking in the Way – A Devotional Journey Through the Scriptures Jesus Read

by Toby Shockey

Copyright © 2021. All rights reserved, including the right to reproduce this book or portions thereof in any form whatsoever. Toby Shockey

For information, contact the author at:
www.tobyshockey.com or www.mountaintime.org

ISBN: 979-8-9857349-6-6

Riverstone Group Publishing

Manufactured in the United States of America

Photo of the author by Nico Zinsmeyer

Unless otherwise noted, all Scripture quotations are from The Holy Bible, English Standard Version. ESV® Text Edition: 2016. Copyright © 2001 by Crossway Bibles, a publishing ministry of Good News Publishers

CONTENTS

Foreword 7
Introduction 11
1. Genesis: Mercy from the Start 14
2. Exodus: A Cry for Help 17
3. Leviticus: Better Than a Goat 20
4. Numbers: Hearing the Voices 23
5. Deuteronomy: Suspended and Sustained 26
6. Joshua: The Battle Is Already Won 29
7. Judges: When God Is Done 33
8. Ruth: Bitter and Better Days 36
9. 1 Samuel: Don't Take the Shortcut 40
10. 2 Samuel: When the Answer Is No 43
11. 1 Kings: Make Up Your Mind 47
12. 2 Kings: Don't You Know I'm Important? 50
13. 1 Chronicles: Significance in Insignificance 53
14. 2 Chronicles: Falling at the Finish Line 56
15. Ezra: The kings and the King 59
16. Nehemiah: The Tools of Opposition 62
17. Esther: When Bitterness Takes Hold 65
18. Job: When the Sky Is Falling 68
19. Psalms: When God Is Taking Too Long 72
20. Proverbs: Wisdom with Words 76
21. Ecclesiastes: The Illusion of Control 79
22. Song of Solomon: God Gives Good Gifts 82
23. Isaiah: What Might Have Been 85

24. Jeremiah: Don't Follow Your Heart 88
25. Lamentations: Hope in the Rubble 91
26. Ezekiel: Coming to Life 94
27. Daniel: The Conquering Captive 98
28. Hosea: What's in a Name? 101
29. Joel: When God Comes to Stay 105
30. Amos: Don't Shoot the Messenger 108
31. Obadiah: Who Cares? 111
32. Jonah: When God Loves Your Enemies 114
33. Micah: Light in the Darkness 118
34. Nahum: God Is Who He Is 121
35. Habakkuk: Watching and Waiting 124
36. Zephaniah: The Purging of Pride 128
37. Haggai: When God Gets in Your Way 131
38. Zechariah: His Part, Our Part 134
39. Malachi: *How* Have You Loved Us? 137
40. Looking Back: That We Might Have Hope 141

FOREWORD

Optical illusions. You know, those drawings, images or objects that cause us to think that we see something that's not there or fail to see something that actually is there. There are many types of these visual illusions, and I'm intrigued by many of the ones that I've experienced over the years. You're probably familiar with that well-known sketch by W. E. Hill that is either a young girl or an old woman. Or is the sketch *both* simultaneously? The same drawing can be observed in two entirely different ways.

How about examples of when our eyes are overstimulated and then our brain interprets the data — only to discover, upon closer inspection, that what we thought we saw does not (or cannot) actually exist? Like the blurry "afterimages" of floating spots that occur after a camera flash. We perceive them to be there, but they're not actually real. Again, optical illusions cause us to think that we see something that's not there or fail to see something that actually is there.

For some of us, at least a portion (hopefully, a small portion) of what we may have learned through the years about the Old Testament could be compared to an optical illusion. We believe that we see something in the Old Testament that is not there or fail to see something in the Old Testament that actually is there. For example, some may believe that the phrase "God helps those who help themselves" is one of the Ten Commandments. That's believing that something is in the Old Testament that just is not there.

Then there are those who are simply unaware that there are Old Testament Scriptures, many, in fact, that speak specifically and prophetically about the New Testament coming of Jesus Christ. (Several verses found in Isaiah 53 are just an example.) That, of course, is failing to see something in the Old Testament that is actually there.

Biblical "optical illusions" may be common, but they are spiritually unhealthy. Whenever we think we see something in the Old Testament that is not there or fail to see something in the Old Testament that actually is there, we should be quick and ready to repent. And, by the way, the word "repent" is a really good word.

I've known Toby Shockey for most of his life — literally. We met when he was in high school and I was in my late twenties and traveling in ministry full-time. That was 35 years ago. For these three-and-a-half decades now, Toby has been used of the Lord to aid me in experiencing the Bible from a fresh perspective, especially in the Old Testament.

This became notably apparent several years ago when he and I were part of a small group that would meet weekly over breakfast to hold each other accountable and discuss a book we were reading. After a few years and several book selections, the group decided we should take a year and read through the Bible together. So we took our Bibles, our journals and a popular Bible reading plan; and we began. We committed to read our Bibles and journal our insights daily on our own. Then, once a week, we would all meet at a restaurant for breakfast, take time to read our Bibles and journal our insights around the restaurant table.

After about 40 minutes of silent reading and writing, we would then go around the table, one by one, reading our journal entries out loud to the group. We were amazed and encouraged to discover what stood out to each individual person from the exact same passages on our Bible reading plan. This went on for a few years and proved to be life changing for most, if not all of us, in the group.

As I mentioned previously, I began to notice something as we met week by week. I observed that Toby had a particular ability to uncover unique insights from the Old Testament passages that we were all reading. Reading from his journal entries, he would disclose some profound "nuggets" found in a passage that had not caught my attention during my reading of the same verses. Although I may not have stated it this way back then, those were times when the Lord would use Toby to reveal some Biblical "optical illusions" in my thinking and in my theology. Those were times when I was quick and ready to repent.

(For that and many other things, Toby, I remain grateful.)

So, as you read *Walking in the Way: A Devotional Journey Through the Scriptures Jesus Read*, I pray that you will discover some of the same profound "nuggets" that were disclosed to me and that small group around the restaurant table all those years ago.

And may Toby Shockey be used of the Lord in your life to reveal any Biblical "optical illusions" in your thinking and in your theology.

Then ". . .your ears shall hear a word behind you, saying, 'This is the way, walk in it,' when you turn to the right or when you turn to the left" (Isaiah 30:21, English Standard Version).

Walking in the Way,
David Guion
The Country Church, Marion, Texas

INTRODUCTION

"I believe every word of the Bible."

"I believe the Bible from the Table of Contents to the maps."

"God said it. I believe it. That settles it."

We can appreciate the heart and sentiment behind each of those statements and others like them because we really do believe that the Bible is truly the Word of God. Both the Old and New Testaments reveal the truth about God and how He has made Himself known to us in Jesus. The Bible isn't our God; but the Scriptures give us the truth about God, the world He created and ourselves.

But while we believe and would fervently argue that the Bible is the Word of God, have we read the Bible that we believe? Several years ago, members of the United States Congress were mocked because they were attempting to pass a national health care bill admittedly without having read what was in the bill. Apparently, the proposal was thousands of pages long; and certain members declared that it was necessary to pass the bill, *so they could know what was in the bill.* In a similar way, sometimes we are presented with a painfully long customer service agreement that requires our signature. Most of us would never consider reading all of the fine print. We just sign or click that we agree and hope for the best. Who has time to read all that?

The point is **not** that the Bible isn't true until we have read every word. In fact, the Bible is God's Word even if we haven't read *any* of it. (And with all due respect to the bumper sticker, what God has said is *already* settled — whether we believe it or not.) For the sake of integrity, we should read the Bible — the whole Bible. There are plenty of great Bible reading plans to help you read through the entire Bible in a year. If that still sounds intimidating, did you know that you can read just three or four chapters each day and read the entire Bible in a year?

More importantly, the truths of God's Word don't help us if we aren't exposed to them — anymore than nutritious foods don't nourish us if we don't consume them. The Bible God gave us includes 66 books; so we should read, study and treasure all 66 books. But you may already realize that this presents some challenges, particularly with the Old Testament. After all, it's *old*. There are verses, chapters and even whole books of the Old Testament that are hard to understand and lengthy sections that are not all that inspiring. Many people have set out to read the whole Bible — only to give up after getting bogged down a few weeks later in the fascinating ritual cleansing descriptions in Leviticus.

Walking in the Way is the second book in a series of Old Testament devotions written to help readers gain exposure to the Old Testament, including some of the more difficult and obscure sections. The first book is entitled *Ancient Paths: Light and Life from the Scriptures Jesus Read*. This second volume is similar in theme but covers all 39 books from the Old Testament with the goal of whetting the appetite for more.

Naturally, you might still be wondering, "Why the Old Testament?" Well, the main reason is that the Old Testament points to Jesus and is only understood in the light of Jesus. Not only is Jesus predicted and promised, but the story of God's people reveals their desperate need for a Savior — and ours! Related to that, the Old Testament is as much the Word of God as the New Testament. The Bible that Jesus and all of the New Testament writers read was the *Old* Testament. Our understanding of the New Testament is deeper and richer through the study of the Old. Those who set their minds and hearts to read and study the Old Testament have come to love it. We read and study the Old Testament because these 39 books are powerful, relevant and life changing.

The title for this devotional book is *Walking in the Way*, which comes from Isaiah 30:20–21, "And though the Lord give you the bread of adversity and the water of affliction, yet your Teacher will not hide himself anymore, but your eyes shall see your Teacher. And your ears shall hear a word behind you, saying, 'This is the way, walk in it,' when you turn to the right or when you turn to the left." When we spend time in God's Word, we learn to hear His voice as He leads us in the way we should go. The Holy Spirit can speak to us without a chapter and verse from Scripture, but we will find that He often reveals His will and His heart to us as we spend time reading and savoring His Word.

Thank you for choosing to at least begin this journey through each book of the Old Testament. I know that you will be blessed and fed by the words of Scripture. My prayer is that the additional devotional thoughts will offer a measure of insight and inspire you to love God's Word and, more importantly, love God Himself more deeply and intently. May you continually hear His voice saying to you, "This is the way, walk in it."

–Toby Shockey
www.mountaintime.org
www.tobyshockey.com

DAY 1

GENESIS: MERCY FROM THE START
READING: GENESIS 2-3.

FOCUS: *The LORD God said to the serpent, "Because you have done this, cursed are you above all livestock and above all beasts of the field; on your belly you shall go, and dust you shall eat all the days of your life. I will put enmity between you and the woman, and between your offspring and her offspring; he shall bruise your head, and you shall bruise his heel." To the woman he said, "I will surely multiply your pain in childbearing; in pain you shall bring forth children. Your desire shall be contrary to your husband, but he shall rule over you." And to Adam he said, "Because you have listened to the voice of your wife and have eaten of the tree of which I commanded you, 'You shall not eat of it,' cursed is the ground because of you; in pain you shall eat of it all the days of your life; thorns and thistles it shall bring forth for you; and you shall eat the plants of the field. By the sweat of your face you shall eat bread, till you return to the ground, for out of it you were taken; for you are dust, and to dust you shall return." The man called his wife's name Eve, because she was the mother of all living. And the LORD God made for Adam and for his wife garments of skins and clothed them.*

Genesis 3:14–21

Since the story of Adam and Eve is so familiar to many of us, we might miss some of the details when we assume that we already know what happens. But here's a seemingly easy Bible trivia question: What was the name of Adam's wife in Genesis 1 and 2? We might assume the answer is, of course, Eve. But "Eve" doesn't become Eve until almost the end of Genesis 3. Up until that point, she doesn't have a name and is only called "the woman" or "a helper." In fact, even Adam doesn't get his name until late in Genesis 2; and there the

Hebrew word for "Adam" (which is Adam) also could be translated as "the man" instead of a proper name.

So why do the names matter, especially for Eve? Generally, names in the Bible are important, with a significant meaning attached to a person's name. Often the meaning of a person's name actually played out in how they responded to situations in life. Eve was given her name by Adam because she was the mother of all the living. The name Eve literally means "life-giver." While the meaning of the name is important, even more significant is the timing. Before Adam gave Eve her name, they had just finished literally ruining everything! Eve believed the lies and deceptions of the serpent and ate some of the forbidden fruit. And Adam was right there beside her, also eating the forbidden fruit. With that, Adam and Eve broke the world; and things have never been the same.

Was it really that difficult to not eat the fruit of one tree when all the others were available to them? Why didn't God simply choose to not include the tree in the Garden? We can raise plenty of questions about what happened, but none of them change the outcome. The astonishing part of the story, however, is not their failure but God's mercy. He knew what they were going to do, and He knew exactly when they ignored Him and ate the fruit. Nothing they did took God by surprise, but He still pursued them anyway. No silent treatment, no probationary "cooling off" period — just mercy. He knew exactly where they were and came looking for them.

Yes, there were dire consequences, not because God was spiteful or vindictive, but rather because things could never be the same. Even as Adam blamed Eve and Eve blamed the serpent, when God spoke, there was a foreshadowing of redemption when the serpent's head would be crushed one day. But even before Adam and Eve were banished from the Garden of Eden, Adam somehow realized that God was merciful. God could have destroyed them, but He was allowing them to live — even if they were moving to the east.

Eve only became Eve after she and Adam had ruined the world. But Adam gave her the name Eve because they were not destroyed and would go on to be givers of life. Pain and toil and futility would be a part of the world they were entering, but God wasn't abandoning them. Now that they saw the need, the Lord even clothed them. Sometimes we like to point fingers at Adam and Eve and say, "If only they hadn't sinned…"; but in their story and especially in their failure, we see the first evidence of God's great mercy. Obviously, sin only has increased since Adam and Eve's original sin; but one day, the mercy God showed to Adam and Eve and His heart of forgiveness towards His children would be revealed fully in Jesus.

HEAD TO HEART

- Do you know the meaning of your name, or does your name have a special significance?

- In what ways has God come looking for you when you might have been trying to get away from Him?

- How have you seen God's mercy — even in the consequences of your sin?

DAY 2

EXODUS: A CRY FOR HELP
READING: EXODUS 1-2.

FOCUS: *During those many days the king of Egypt died, and the people of Israel groaned because of their slavery and cried out for help. Their cry for rescue from slavery came up to God. And God heard their groaning, and God remembered his covenant with Abraham, with Isaac, and with Jacob. God saw the people of Israel—and God knew.*

Exodus 2:23-25

God is never in a hurry. What He says He will do is exactly what He will do. But by our standards, over 400 years is a long time of waiting. Think about all of the descendants of Abraham who lived and died during this period while the promises God had made to Abraham were still in the process of being fulfilled. (Genesis 12:1-4, 15:13) From Abraham to Isaac to Jacob to Joseph and his brothers ending up in Egypt, a multitude of days had passed. The generations of Abraham's offspring had done their part to be fruitful and multiply — only to become Pharaoh's slave work force.

At the beginning of Exodus, we see a glimmer of hope in the circumstances surrounding the birth of Moses; but just when it seemed like things were looking up, the man God selected was on his way to the wilderness for the next 40 years. (Exodus 2:11-22; Acts 7:30) Even after Moses was born, another *80 years* would pass before an Exodus would be discussed. (Exodus 7:7) God doesn't do things the way that we would do them or at the pace we would choose.

The people groaned and cried out for help. And God heard. God remembered. God saw. And God knew. Our first thought might be, "Well, of course, He did those things"; but there is something deliberate in the way that Moses (the author of Exodus) chose each of those verbs in succession.

God didn't *hear* their cries as though they were background noise or a few voices among millions. He listened. He tuned attentively to their cries.

God didn't *remember* them as if He had forgotten or lost track of them and the memory of them suddenly came back. He was mindful of them in the sense that He was ready to act on their behalf.

God didn't *see* them as though He had a vague awareness that they were there. He saw them in the sense that He turned His eyes to them and gazed. His attention was directed towards them for their good.

God didn't *know* them in the sense of a casual acquaintance or in the way we know facts and information. He *knew* them in the sense of intimacy and relationship, and He *knew* their situation.

These words offer tremendous comfort. Think of Moses many years later, having finally left Egypt, having miraculously crossed the Red Sea, having seen God's provision again and again in the wilderness, compiling the story and thinking back to God's response to the cries of His people. Many years had passed, but God indeed had kept all of His promises.

You may be living in your own version of Egypt today, and you may be crying out for help. Maybe you've been crying out for a long time, and now you are weary of waiting. His timing is clearly not like ours, but know this today:

God hears you.

God remembers you.

God sees you.

And God knows you and your affliction.

He can't be predicted, but He can be trusted. We don't know His timing, but we can trust His ways.

HEAD TO HEART

- Why does it seem as though God takes so long to answer some prayers?

- Do you sometimes stop praying because there seems to be no answer?

- Will you trust that He hears, remembers, sees and knows — even as you continue to wait?

DAY 3

LEVITICUS: BETTER THAN A GOAT
READING: LEVITICUS 16.

FOCUS: *Then he shall kill the goat of the sin offering that is for the people and bring its blood inside the veil and do with its blood as he did with the blood of the bull, sprinkling it over the mercy seat and in front of the mercy seat. Thus he shall make atonement for the Holy Place, because of the uncleannesses of the people of Israel and because of their transgressions, all their sins. And so he shall do for the tent of meeting, which dwells with them in the midst of their uncleannesses…And when he has made an end of atoning for the Holy Place and the tent of meeting and the altar, he shall present the live goat. And Aaron shall lay both his hands on the head of the live goat, and confess over it all the iniquities of the people of Israel, and all their transgressions, all their sins. And he shall put them on the head of the goat and send it away into the wilderness by the hand of a man who is in readiness. The goat shall bear all their iniquities on itself to a remote area, and he shall let the goat go free in the wilderness.*

Leviticus 16:15-16, 20-22

When was the last time you read a devotion from Leviticus? Now having read the passage, you might have been reminded why you probably haven't spent an excessive amount of time in this book of laws. One of the benefits of reading from Leviticus is simply to be reminded of how much better the new covenant is than the old. Salvation is by grace through faith in Jesus, not by keeping a set of laws.

This passage describes some of the things that were carried out by the high priest on the Day of Atonement (Yom Kippur). The sons of Aaron had learned the hard way that the purification rituals were to be taken seriously (Leviticus 10:1-3) and carried out exactly the way specified by God. The Day of Atonement was a holy and solemn occasion.

This specific portion of the Day of Atonement involved two goats: one was killed and its blood shed for the sins of the people; while the other was set free into the wilderness, which represented the removal of their sins. (Here is the origin of referring to someone as a scapegoat, the one who takes the blame.) This was only part of the Day of Atonement practice since additional sacrifices were made on other occasions.

All the while knowing that He one day would send His Son to fulfill the Law, God instituted the Old Testament sacrificial and legal systems by which His people were to be set apart. While much of that system is strange to a person reading the Bible today, these Old Testament rituals point forward to Jesus and remind us why God sent His Son.

Jesus later said, "Do not think that I have come to abolish the Law or the Prophets; I have not come to abolish them but to fulfill them" (Matthew 5:17). If Jesus didn't abolish the Old Testament Law, then why do we not make sacrifices today? Nothing changed about God's requirements. Righteousness and holiness were still the standard; and the entire Old Testament demonstrates that people, even God's chosen people, were utterly incapable of doing or being what God required. Jesus didn't abolish the Law – He fulfilled the Law. He did what the Law could never do. He did what they (and of course, we) could never do – achieve our own righteousness or live up to God's standard of holiness.

Jesus came to be the sacrifice who would end the need for any further sacrifices. He was perfect and sinless, and yet He was slaughtered to make atonement for all who would believe in Him. He fulfilled the Law and made the sacrificial system obsolete by becoming the ultimate sacrifice. Nothing else is needed. Transgressions were punished and mercy was shown all at the same time by the sacrifice that only He was able to offer.

Hebrews 10:1 says, "For since the law has but a shadow of the good things to come instead of the true form of these realities, it can never, by the same sacrifices that are continually offered every year, make perfect those who draw near." Even when the people offered the sacrifices, they still had to keep offering them year after year. They were never justified, once and for all, by offering goats. "For it is impossible for the blood of bulls and goats to take away sins" (Hebrews 10:4). The atonement rituals were necessary but never permanent.

But Jesus accomplished our atonement once and for all. We are permanently made right with God through Jesus. "And every priest stands daily at his service, offering repeatedly the same sacrifices, which can never take away sins. But when Christ had offered for all time a single sacrifice for sins, he sat down at the right hand of God, waiting from that time until his enemies should be made a footstool for his feet" (Hebrews 10:11–13). Jesus sat down at the right hand of God because His work of making us right with God by His own sacrifice is done. "It is finished" (John 19:30).

On this side of heaven, we are reconciled completely to God, but we still are being made to be like Him each day. Our standing is righteousness, but often our living falls woefully short. We are still in the process of being sanctified (made holy) daily — even though God already has made us completely righteous in Christ. Hebrews 10:14 speaks of this balance: "For by a single offering he has *perfected for all time* those who *are being sanctified.*" (emphasis mine) Jesus did what we – or a goat – could never do.

HEAD TO HEART

- Why would God establish a sacrificial system that never would fully perfect His people?

- What was different about Jesus' sacrifice than all of the sacrifices that had been offered previously?

- How does knowing that you are righteous before God (2 Corinthians 5:21) help you seek to become more and more like Him?

DAY 4

NUMBERS: HEARING THE VOICES
READING: NUMBERS 13.

FOCUS: *At the end of forty days they returned from spying out the land. And they came to Moses and Aaron and to all the congregation of the people of Israel in the wilderness of Paran, at Kadesh. They brought back word to them and to all the congregation, and showed them the fruit of the land. And they told him, "We came to the land to which you sent us. It flows with milk and honey, and this is its fruit…But Caleb quieted the people before Moses and said, "Let us go up at once and occupy it, for we are well able to overcome it." Then the men who had gone up with him said, "We are not able to go up against the people, for they are stronger than we are." So they brought to the people of Israel a bad report of the land that they had spied out, saying, "The land, through which we have gone to spy it out, is a land that devours its inhabitants, and all the people that we saw in it are of great height. And there we saw the Nephilim (the sons of Anak, who come from the Nephilim), and we seemed to ourselves like grasshoppers, and so we seemed to them."*

Numbers 13:25-27, 30-33

The Promised Land was every bit as amazing as the people of Israel had been led to believe, but somehow they had missed the part about having to defeat scary enemies to secure what was theirs. Moses sent 12 spies into the land of Canaan, and they were all in agreement that the land was abundant and flowed with milk and honey. Two of the spies, Joshua and Caleb, were ready to go in and take what God was giving to them; but the other 10 spies were afraid of all the tall people already living there. Even in the Old Testament, nothing is ever easy.

Sadly, fear triumphed over faith that day. Caleb's words of encouragement were ignored. If there were obstacles to entering the land, especially tall obstacles, the people of Israel decided the reward wasn't worth the risk. The flawed logic of the fearful was that, although God had brought them this far in bringing them out of Egypt, rescuing them from Pharaoh's army and continually sustaining them on the journey, He nevertheless was incapable now of giving them victory in the land. Fear caused them to believe that God could not or would not fulfill His promise.

As a result, an unbelieving generation would die in the wilderness and never possess the land that God was giving them. They would not move forward, so their consequence was exactly that – *they would not move forward*. Knowing what God had promised and having heard the encouraging words of Joshua and Caleb, a generation would die off before anyone entered the land — all because the people listened to the wrong voices.

Thousands of years later, you've likely heard those same voices, and they are telling the same lies. "Be afraid — constantly. You're on your own here. The opposition is huge — even bigger than God. Maybe God took care of you in the past, but we're talking about right now. Better play it safe. Don't step out in faith — faith is just too risky. Maybe you didn't hear God right anyway. Can you really trust Him?"

The voice of fear still speaks to us — sometimes softly and other times screaming. You probably won't stop hearing messages of fear, but you don't have to *listen* to them. Trusting what God is saying more than the other voices doesn't come easily. Often the Lord speaks in a still, quiet voice; while the voices of fear and doubt are so loud.

To which voice will you listen? On which voice will you concentrate so that the other is drowned out? Through His Word, through prayer and in Godly counsel, the Holy Spirit will speak to us; but He rarely chooses to raise His voice. More than that, our deliberate effort is required to hear Him above all the noise. While the enemy bombards us with half-truths and outright lies, the Holy Spirit speaks life and peace. When we are tuned in to what the Lord is saying, we can enjoy the blessings of obedience.

HEAD TO HEART

- What do you think were God's purposes in letting the spies see how intimidating were the inhabitants of the land?

- What was different about Joshua and Caleb that caused them to be courageous when the others were afraid?

- What do the voices of fear and discouragement say to you, and how do you contend with them?

DAY 5

DEUTERONOMY: SUSPENDED AND SUSTAINED

READING: DEUTERONOMY 8.

FOCUS: *The whole commandment that I command you today you shall be careful to do, that you may live and multiply, and go in and possess the land that the LORD swore to give to your fathers. And you shall remember the whole way that the LORD your God has led you these forty years in the wilderness, that he might humble you, testing you to know what was in your heart, whether you would keep his commandments or not. And he humbled you and let you hunger and fed you with manna, which you did not know, nor did your fathers know, that he might make you know that man does not live by bread alone, but man lives by every word that comes from the mouth of the LORD. Your clothing did not wear out on you and your foot did not swell these forty years. Know then in your heart that, as a man disciplines his son, the LORD your God disciplines you. So you shall keep the commandments of the LORD your God by walking in his ways and by fearing him.*

Deuteronomy 8:1-6

If you have walked with the Lord for a while now, you probably have noticed along the way that your idea of "soon" and God's are not quite in sync. God is so patient with us in the earlier days of our journey as most of us have dedicated so many prayers and so much energy towards getting God to hurry up and get on board with our agenda. After all, we have plans; or if we really want to sound spiritual, we might say that we have "a vision." Translation: We want something to happen, and God should make it happen — now.

If our plans are from the Lord, they will happen in His way and in His time. If we're trying to advance our agenda and use God in the process, we have some hard lessons ahead of us. God's ways are not our ways, and His thoughts are not ours either. (Isaiah 55:8-9) One of the clearest demonstrations of that truth is how much time God uses to prepare and develop us before He uses us.

To be fair, by the time Moses spoke these words of encouragement and clarity to the Hebrews in the wilderness, they already could have been in the Promised Land for decades. But their unwillingness to trust the Lord demonstrated they weren't ready. Still, 40 years are a long time to wander and wait.

God's people may have considered all that time as wasted since there was a land awaiting them, and they essentially were waiting for the previous generation to die off in the wilderness. But God doesn't waste time, and these years would be formative and instructive for His people. Although they had been slaves in Egypt for as long as anyone could remember, God used the time in the wilderness to humble His people. How did He humble them? He let them hunger. No, they didn't starve or get anywhere close to starving; but they experienced their need for God's provision at a deeper level than they ever had before.

Even as they grumbled and longed for the "good ol' days" when they were slaves in Egypt, God literally rained down food out of the sky. He fed them with manna and provided in the way that He did, so they would learn to look to Him and depend on Him. If they ever forgot that lesson (and oh, how they would forget), pride would destroy them. As they finally prepared to enter the land, they could not deny that they had been sustained by God all those years. Even if they grumbled during the entire season of wilderness wandering, God had provided for them and disciplined them for their good.

Despite Moses' warning and pleadings, the generation that finally would enter the Promised Land with Joshua successfully ignored God, stopped looking to Him and generally failed. The manna had stopped falling, but who needed manna with all the abundance of the land? We're in the land now – God who? God was patient, but they never learned. Will we?

Times have changed, but people haven't; and God still works in similar ways to develop and prepare His people. We're not necessarily about to enter a new land, but there is probably something we've longed for God to do or to provide. Maybe our wait isn't 40 years, but it's been long enough and then some. Maybe no one has to die, but we feel as though we might die from waiting. The parallels between our lives and the people to whom Moses was speaking are striking. We want to move forward, and God wants us to sit still and wait. We want God to prosper and bless us, and He wants to sustain us as we learn to trust Him. We want a new chapter in our lives, but He wants us to learn the lessons from the current chapter first.

But know in your season of waiting that God will sustain you. You will be carried; and as you remain on the path of obedience, you will get through this at some point. Obey the Lord completely in what you know to do today. Learn to be thankful for the "manna" He is providing in this season because the next season will be different. Think of all the times He has sustained you before. Finally, remember everything we undergo in this present life is preparing us for a greater glory in the forever Promised Land. As you wait and as you endure, His grace is sufficient.

HEAD TO HEART

- Why is it easy to see the faithlessness and frailty of the people in the Bible and not nearly as easy to recognize the same things in our own lives?

- Obviously, God could have fed His people with manna forever. Why do you think He stopped? (Joshua 5:12)

- What is God teaching you in the areas in which you are waiting?

DAY 6

JOSHUA:
THE BATTLE IS ALREADY WON
READING: JOSHUA 5-6.

FOCUS: *When Joshua was by Jericho, he lifted up his eyes and looked, and behold, a man was standing before him with his drawn sword in his hand. And Joshua went to him and said to him, "Are you for us, or for our adversaries?" And he said, "No; but I am the commander of the army of the LORD. Now I have come." And Joshua fell on his face to the earth and worshiped and said to him, "What does my lord say to his servant?" And the commander of the LORD's army said to Joshua, "Take off your sandals from your feet, for the place where you are standing is holy." And Joshua did so.*

Now Jericho was shut up inside and outside because of the people of Israel. None went out, and none came in. And the LORD said to Joshua, "See, I have given Jericho into your hand, with its king and mighty men of valor. You shall march around the city, all the men of war going around the city once. Thus shall you do for six days. Seven priests shall bear seven trumpets of rams' horns before the ark. On the seventh day you shall march around the city seven times, and the priests shall blow the trumpets. And when they make a long blast with the ram's horn, when you hear the sound of the trumpet, then all the people shall shout with a great shout, and the wall of the city will fall down flat, and the people shall go up, everyone straight before him."

Joshua 5:13-6:5

As a much younger man, Joshua had seen the land of Canaan before. As he crossed the Jordan River again after a 40-year wait, he likely thought about what could have been. Joshua and Caleb saw the abundance of the land and the way that God would bless His people, but the other 10 spies only could see the size of the current occupants. Fear carried the day, and Joshua wandered and waited in the wilderness with all the others.

But now Moses was gone, and Joshua no longer was in his shadow. After Moses died, God had encouraged Joshua to be strong and courageous and reminded Joshua that He would be with him wherever he would go. (Joshua 1) No doubt, Joshua was indeed strong and courageous; but that didn't make Jericho any less fortified or formidable. When they celebrated the Passover for the first time in Canaan and the manna no longer fell from the sky, there was no going back. The "ships" already had been burned.

As Joshua prepared to begin the occupation of the land, the Lord had something else in store for Joshua. When Joshua encountered a man with a drawn sword, the appearance of the man so impressed him that Joshua had to know if He was on their side. "Are you for us or for our adversaries?"

But the man said, "No." Instead of offering His affiliation, He revealed His identity. He was the commander of the army of the Lord. Now at first, we might assume that He was a warring angel; but He was more than an angel. The Bible doesn't give us many additional details, but Joshua's response reveals what we need to know. Since Joshua fell on his face and worshipped, we can conclude that Joshua was in the presence of Jesus. Before Jesus came to Bethlehem as an infant, He came to Jericho as the commander of the armies of the Lord. Yes, Jesus was born in Bethlehem; but He existed with the Father and the Spirit from before the beginning. He is the Word Who was in the beginning with God because He is God. (John 1:1)

Perhaps expecting some kind of battle instructions, Joshua made known that he was the one who was taking orders in this conversation. What was he told to do? "Joshua, take your shoes off — you're on holy ground." Not only was Joshua in the presence of the Lord, but he would not have missed the significance of being told to remove his sandals. What God had done for Moses when all of this began (Exodus 3), He was now doing for Joshua. If Joshua needed any additional incentive to be strong and courageous, he was receiving that now.

With the presence of Jesus came the assurance of victory. Joshua knew he was walking in obedience to the Lord's command and that he was the man to lead the people, but how would he conquer a city that was tightly shut with high walls? Marching around the city and blowing trumpets might have seemed like a strange strategy, and the men of war might have felt ridiculous walking in circles; but this battle was never about the strategy or tactics.

Because Joshua had seen Jesus and knew that He came not to take sides but to take over, victory was a given. Do we have the same assurance? The battles are different, but the same victory is assured because of Jesus. Just as Jesus won the battle for His people at Jericho, He fought and won the ultimate battle over sin and death on the cross. When He arose, sin and death lost. And because He conquered, we share in His victory. Paul later wrote, "But thanks be to God, who in Christ always leads us in triumphal procession, and through us spreads the fragrance of the knowledge of him everywhere" (2 Corinthians 2:14).

What we see with our eyes doesn't always look like victory – far from it. But that's when we trust in what the Word of God says more than how things appear. The Word says, "No, in all these things we are more than conquerors through him who loved us" (Romans 8:37). Even as we deal with smaller battles, the ultimate battle already is won for us in Christ. Just as the people had to walk (literally) in obedience around the walls of Jericho, so we daily walk in the paths of trust and obedience in full assurance of the outcome. The same Jesus, Who appeared to Joshua as the commander of the army of the Lord, is coming again soon.

HEAD TO HEART

- In what specific areas do you struggle to see yourself as more than a conqueror?

- How do we handle the things in life that seem like losses and defeats if we know that victory is assured?

- What "walls" have you seen fall as you have trusted God and walked in obedience?

DAY 7

JUDGES: WHEN GOD HAS HAD ENOUGH

READING: JUDGES 6:1-6, JUDGES 10:6-16.

FOCUS: *And the people of Israel cried out to the LORD, saying, "We have sinned against you, because we have forsaken our God and have served the Baals." And the LORD said to the people of Israel, "Did I not save you from the Egyptians and from the Amorites, from the Ammonites and from the Philistines? The Sidonians also, and the Amalekites and the Maonites oppressed you, and you cried out to me, and I saved you out of their hand. Yet you have forsaken me and served other gods; therefore I will save you no more. Go and cry out to the gods whom you have chosen; let them save you in the time of your distress." And the people of Israel said to the LORD, "We have sinned; do to us whatever seems good to you. Only please deliver us this day." So they put away the foreign gods from among them and served the LORD, and he became impatient over the misery of Israel.*

Judges 10:10-16

One of the things that always set Yahweh apart from the false gods of the other nations was that He always refused to share His right to be God with anyone or anything else. The way He demanded exclusive loyalty and worship from His people would lead us to believe that God truly did see Himself as Lord of all. Why is God so opposed to idolatry? Why will He not share His rightful place with anyone else? Why does He expect His people to worship Him and Him only? *Because God knows Who He is.* We would expect nothing less from the one, true God.

By their own choosing and failure, God's people continually were surrounded and influenced by the idolatry of the other nations. Having failed to drive the inhabitants out of the land that God intended for

His people to occupy by themselves, the people who remained caused Israel to fall into idolatry — the very reason why God had wanted them to be ousted in the first place. God's commands are not random or arbitrary but given to us for good reasons — even if we don't fully understand those reasons.

The book of Judges describes the resulting monotonous cycle. God blessed His people until they grew fat and happy, and then they would forget about God and turn to the false gods of the other nations. God would allow His people eventually to be enslaved and oppressed by these nations until they became so miserable that they finally would cry out to God again. This pattern was repeated over and over again; but with every cycle, Israel spiraled to a new low and further away from the Lord.

After the latest round of idolatry leading to oppression, this time at the hands of the Ammonites, the people of Israel finally and predictably cried out to the Lord for rescue. The Lord's response this time was not what they would have predicted. "Remember all those other times I saved you? Still, you keep returning to your idols. I'm done rescuing you." That was obviously not a good place to be, but the Lord continued, "Go and cry out to the gods whom you have chosen; let them save you in the time of your distress." God was, as we say, *done*.

Of course, they wanted to be rescued out of the situation they had created for themselves; but God knows the difference between someone wanting Him or merely wanting His help. Yahweh would not be used or manipulated in the way that idolaters bargain and negotiate with their gods in the vain effort to get them to act. Despite the hardness of their hearts, evidently God got His point across to them. They knew they truly had crossed the line. "We have sinned; do to us whatever seems good to you. Only please deliver us this day." Would this cry for help be any different than all the others?

Thankfully, the people of Israel did two things right this time. First, asking Him to do to them as He saw fit was a measure of surrender.

They wanted Him — even if that entailed suffering consequences as well. We know that because, secondly, they put away their idols and served the Lord. Their repentance reflected an actual turning away from sin, not just regretting the consequences. What was God's response? Impatience. But the people of Israel no doubt were relieved that God was impatient because His impatience was due to their misery. Although their misery was self-inflicted and their consequences well deserved, God took no pleasure in their suffering. God was just and righteous, but He also was merciful.

While there were a few good but fleeting moments, God's people continued to sin and turn to idols. He was too holy to ignore their sin but too merciful not to rescue them out of their affliction. The continual failure of God's people was leading to an ultimate solution — one that was prepared by God *before* His people ever sinned. Jesus would suffer the wrath of God on the cross so that God would be just in punishing sin *and* gloriously merciful to those who trust in Him. (Romans 3:21-26) As we strive for holiness and surrender our will to His, in Christ we never need to fear God reaching the place where He is done with us. (Romans 8:1) God is never done with us because, after all, "it is finished" (John 19:30).

HEAD TO HEART

- What are some of the false gods you have identified in your life? When you don't run to God, to whom or what do you run?

- Do you ever feel as though you might have "out-sinned" God's mercy? Why is this not possible?

- What is the difference between true repentance and "crocodile tears"?

DAY 8

RUTH: BITTER AND BETTER DAYS
READING: RUTH 1.

FOCUS: *But Ruth said, "Do not urge me to leave you or to return from following you. For where you go I will go, and where you lodge I will lodge. Your people shall be my people, and your God my God. Where you die I will die, and there will I be buried. May the LORD do so to me and more also if anything but death parts me from you." And when Naomi saw that she was determined to go with her, she said no more. So the two of them went on until they came to Bethlehem. And when they came to Bethlehem, the whole town was stirred because of them. And the women said, "Is this Naomi?" She said to them, "Do not call me Naomi; call me Mara, for the Almighty has dealt very bitterly with me. I went away full, and the LORD has brought me back empty. Why call me Naomi, when the LORD has testified against me and the Almighty has brought calamity upon me?" So Naomi returned, and Ruth the Moabite her daughter-in-law with her, who returned from the country of Moab. And they came to Bethlehem at the beginning of barley harvest.*

Ruth 1:16-22

Naomi was having a rough time, and we can understand why she was so bitter. Having lost her husband and two sons must have been unimaginably hard; but Naomi, whose name meant "pleasant," was less than pleasant as she arrived back in Bethlehem. The road home hadn't been an easy one, and she hadn't expected to travel the road back to Bethlehem without her family. Naomi was bitter, but she also was *wrong*.

Perhaps that sounds harsh – given her circumstances; and of course, telling Naomi that she was wrong would not have been advisable. You may have noticed that people who already are angry and bitter don't appreciate being told that they also are wrong. However, we can learn from God's dealings with Naomi and her response since we all have or will have some bitter chapters in our lives. Such is life in a broken world, and Naomi knew that reality all too well. Maybe you do, too.

But let's consider some things about Naomi's situation. First, God hadn't led them to Moab when there was a famine in Israel. Going to Moab was their choice. As best we can tell, Naomi's late husband Elimelech panicked and took matters into his own hands by taking his family to Moab. We often make the worst choices when we go where we aren't supposed to go. Related to that, God didn't lead either Israelite son to marry Moabite women. Marrying outside the faith not only was forbidden but also was just a bad idea. The Moabites were idolaters and continual enemies of Israel. (For the inglorious origins of the Moabites and Ammonites, see Genesis 19.) And yet one of these Moabite women was none other than Ruth.

We don't know how or why, but Elimelech and the two sons died in Moab; and only Naomi, Orpah and Ruth remained. Obviously, things went badly for Naomi in Moab; and there was nothing left to do but go back home. Bethlehem only served to remind Naomi of all that she had lost. As much as we might sympathize with Naomi's outlook, her bitterness prevented Naomi from seeing what God was doing and the blessings He already had granted her. (Aren't you glad we never do that?)

First, Naomi misinterpreted the situation. Her pain, although justified, caused her to assume that God had turned against her. Her words conveyed that she essentially considered herself cursed. But was she really? Having sadness and loss in our lives is not the same as being cursed by God. When we are hurting – as Naomi certainly was, we tend to see only through our pain, which is why a time of mourning is not the time to make important decisions. Given more time to grieve or vent, we probably will have a better perspective later.

Secondly, Naomi overlooked the blessings she already had. Naomi and Ruth came to Bethlehem at the beginning of the barley harvest. Obviously, that meant there finally was a harvest. The famine they once had fled now was finally over. Even more importantly, Naomi seemingly did not appreciate the loyalty and support being shown to her by Ruth. Let's be honest: Would you have stayed with your *mother-in-law* under the same circumstances? Ruth was a blessing that Naomi was not appreciating at this point. Sometimes our blessings are obvious, but we fail to appreciate them.

Finally, Naomi underestimated the ability of God to bring joy out of sorrow. Of course, Naomi could not have known about the joy that God was going to bring out of the sorrow. God was in the process of doing something much bigger than she could have understood. Ruth would meet Boaz who would redeem Ruth just as God was redeeming the entire situation. We all love a happy ending, but the glorious scene of Naomi holding her adoptive grandson came only after a bitter struggle. "Then Naomi took the child and laid him on her lap and became his nurse. And the women of the neighborhood gave him a name, saying, 'A son has been born to Naomi.' They named him Obed. He was the father of Jesse, the father of David" (Ruth 4:16–17).

Naomi didn't know that her daughter-in-law would be the great-grandmother to King David and the ancestor of all the kings of Judah. She also didn't know that the Son of God would be born into that same lineage many years later. (Matthew 1:1-17) With that in mind, we don't know many important things about our lives either. Bitter days surely happen; but better days happen, too. We don't have to pretend that everything is just peachy in an awful season, but we can remember how the Lord remembered Naomi and many others in equally painful situations. Our story is still being written, and the difficult chapter in which we find ourselves now is only a small part of the overall story. Bitterness is easy, but we'll thankfully find out someday that we were wrong. In the bitter days and the better days, God is good.

HEAD TO HEART

- How do we determine the line between appropriately grieving and accusing God of wrongdoing?

- Has there been a time when you were frustrated with God — only to find out you were mistaken?

- In what ways have you created more problems for yourself by trying to avoid suffering or inconvenience at all costs?

DAY 9

1 SAMUEL: DON'T TAKE THE SHORTCUT

READING: 1 SAMUEL 24.

FOCUS: *When Saul returned from following the Philistines, he was told, "Behold, David is in the wilderness of Engedi." Then Saul took three thousand chosen men out of all Israel and went to seek David and his men in front of the Wildgoats' Rocks. And he came to the sheepfolds by the way, where there was a cave, and Saul went in to relieve himself. Now David and his men were sitting in the innermost parts of the cave. And the men of David said to him, "Here is the day of which the LORD said to you, 'Behold, I will give your enemy into your hand, and you shall do to him as it shall seem good to you.'" Then David arose and stealthily cut off a corner of Saul's robe. And afterward David's heart struck him, because he had cut off a corner of Saul's robe. He said to his men, "The LORD forbid that I should do this thing to my lord, the LORD's anointed, to put out my hand against him, seeing he is the LORD's anointed." So David persuaded his men with these words and did not permit them to attack Saul. And Saul rose up and left the cave and went on his way.*

1 Samuel 24:1-7

David certainly had the opportunity. With the thrust of a sword, David could have ended Saul's quest to murder him, humiliated his enemy and stepped into the role of king that God already had promised him. But David refused to take the shortcut. Why? King Saul was truly a lame duck by this point, having already been rejected as king by the Lord because of his disobedience. (1 Samuel 15) In contrast, David was anointed as the next king – even as Saul still held the title.

If David had listened to his companions, he would have done a little "carpe diem" and put Saul out of everyone's misery. The scene in the cave so vividly demonstrated what was happening on a larger scale in the world outside. In both places, David had the advantage and momentum, while Saul was. . . well. . . ahem. . . seeking relief. (The Hebrew term means that Saul literally "covered his feet" while there in the cave.)

Driven by a jealous resentment, Saul had put David through the ringer, throwing spears at him and chasing him all over the land. Similarly, maybe you've noticed that there are people who simply don't like you and for no good reason. No one could say that David's potential revenge had not been provoked. David could have ended Saul and humiliated him in the process, which many would have seen as a fitting end for a deranged king. Imagine the headlines in The Jerusalem Times the next day: "King Slain in Bowels of Cave" or maybe "King De-Throned by Rival" or "Nature Calls — King Falls." What a way to go!

But doing the right thing is sometimes really inconvenient. David restrained himself — despite the counsel of his companions because, for all his faults and insane rage, King Saul was God's anointed. That being the case, only God should bring about Saul's demise — not David or anyone else. David indeed would be the next king but only in God's way and in God's timing.

We might sympathize with David in simply cutting off the corner of Saul's robe when he was. . . well. . . vulnerable, but David quickly realized he effectively was just showing up God's anointed. Sadly, David's swatch of proof ultimately didn't prevent Saul from continuing his pursuit to kill David.

And here is a hard but often-repeated lesson from King Saul: God's anointed doesn't always act the way a person anointed by God should act. The hypocrisy and inconsistency are painfully present. Sometimes the emperor truly isn't wearing any clothes. You may well be assessing a similar situation in your life correctly, but then your role is to trust God and pray rather than criticize and undermine.

David had to be especially careful because, in tearing down Saul, he was elevating himself. If God truly had anointed David to be king, God would establish David as king. *We will never have to violate God's commandments to achieve God's purposes.* Sometimes, however, we have to wait... and trust... and endure. God will do what He has said and what He has purposed but probably not in our timing or in our way.

More than likely, shortcuts will present themselves as God is preparing you for the future He has planned; but shortcuts won't get you where you want to go. For David, killing Saul would have made him just like Saul, the man whom God already had rejected. We often want to simply get where we're going, even spiritually, without allowing God to develop our character and our ability to trust Him along the way. The process of preparation is long and difficult on purpose. Don't take that shortcut, and you'll get where God has prepared for you to be.

HEAD TO HEART

- When we trust in God's overall plan, why do we still struggle to trust His timing?

- In what ways have you been in a situation such as David's and tempted to take matters into your own hands?

- How does a person who is "God's anointed" become like King Saul? Could this happen to you?

DAY 10

2 SAMUEL: WHEN THE ANSWER IS NO

READING: 2 SAMUEL 7.

FOCUS: *Then King David went in and sat before the LORD and said, "Who am I, O Lord GOD, and what is my house, that you have brought me thus far? And yet this was a small thing in your eyes, O Lord GOD. You have spoken also of your servant's house for a great while to come, and this is instruction for mankind, O Lord GOD! And what more can David say to you? For you know your servant, O Lord GOD! Because of your promise, and according to your own heart, you have brought about all this greatness, to make your servant know it. Therefore you are great, O LORD God. For there is none like you, and there is no God besides you, according to all that we have heard with our ears. And who is like your people Israel, the one nation on earth whom God went to redeem to be his people, making himself a name and doing for them great and awesome things by driving out before your people, whom you redeemed for yourself from Egypt, a nation and its gods? And you established for yourself your people Israel to be your people forever. And you, O LORD, became their God. And now, O LORD God, confirm forever the word that you have spoken concerning your servant and concerning his house, and do as you have spoken. And your name will be magnified forever, saying, 'The LORD of hosts is God over Israel,' and the house of your servant David will be established before you. For you, O LORD of hosts, the God of Israel, have made this revelation to your servant, saying, 'I will build you a house.' Therefore your servant has found courage to pray this prayer to you. And now, O Lord GOD, you are God, and your words are true, and you have promised this good thing to your servant. Now therefore may it please you to bless the house of your servant, so that it may continue forever before you. For you, O Lord GOD, have spoken, and with your blessing shall the house of your servant be blessed forever."*

2 Samuel 7:18-29

One of the least enjoyable aspects of life on this planet is being told "no." Even when the issue is not even terribly important, the word "no" stings, annoys and even infuriates. We know and believe that God is love and that He has all wisdom; but even from God, we surely don't like hearing the word "no." Sometimes this is because we are petulant, little children; but other times, our desire is right but misdirected. We can want to do the right thing for the right reason, but that doesn't mean what we want is necessarily God's will.

King David certainly had some bad moments, and the Bible does not hide these from us; but this series of events would make the highlight reel of David's life. Here we get a glimpse of *why* David was called a man after God's own heart. And of all things, David's heart was revealed when God told him "no." After a long and truly eventful wait and preparation process, God had established David as king over Israel. David was truly God's anointed. But soon David realized that he was living it up in a nice home that was made of cedar while the Ark of the Covenant still resided in a tent. After all, the people of Israel were no longer wandering in the Wilderness; so the place of meeting with God no longer needed to be portable. David wanted to build a house for God; and this was a noble, honorable ambition — until God said "no."

God revealed to the prophet Nathan that David was not the one to build the Temple. If David were seeking to make a name for himself, he probably would not have responded in that way. God wanted David to be assured of two things. First, one of his offspring would be the one to build the Temple after David had lived out his days. Interestingly enough, that offspring would be Solomon who was born to David and Bathsheba. (2 Samuel 11-12) Secondly, and more importantly, God was saying to David, "You wanted to build a house for Me, but instead I'm going to build a house for you." God's promise was bigger than David could have expected: "And your house and your kingdom shall be made sure forever before me. Your throne shall be established forever" (2 Samuel 7:16). David's "house" would be a dynasty of kings in Judah that ultimately would culminate in the King of kings and Lord of lords.

Sometimes we want to do something or be something for the Lord, and our desire is noble. We set out to serve the Lord because there are needs to be met and things to be done. But then we seemingly run into a brick wall. We can always expect difficulty and opposition in serving the Lord and His people, but we should never assume that our desire to do something and God's will are necessarily the same thing. Now if we're completely honest, we know that we can disguise our selfish ambition in spiritual terms. We can be attempting to make a name for ourselves or make much of ourselves while claiming that our efforts are all for the Lord.

How can we weigh our motives? How can we seek to know that we're truly serving the Lord and not ourselves? When God inexplicably says no, our response will reveal our motivation. David uttered no complaints and humbly praised the Lord for all His goodness to him. "Who am I?" was the right question. No sense of entitlement, no demands for an explanation. God's grace and goodness are seen — even when the answer isn't the one we wanted.

But if we will humble ourselves to accept God's no and wait for God's timing, we will get to learn what God's will is rather than what God's will isn't. For example, Paul wanted to go to Asia to preach the Gospel; but the Holy Spirit said "no." Paul tried to go to Bithynia for the same reason but got the same result. Surely, he wondered why — until the Spirit clearly revealed that Paul's next assignment was in Macedonia. (Acts 16:6-10) Like perhaps we already have done, Paul could have pushed ahead anyway and went where he wasn't supposed to go because he could see no reason why not. David could have attempted to build the Temple anyway. But in both cases, God was doing something different and something better.

God has plans for you. As His workmanship (the Greek word from which we get the word "poem"), He has specific things for you to do. (Ephesians 2:10) If you're getting a "no" right now, there is something better. Trust His heart. Trust His timing. Then serve the Lord with gladness.

HEAD TO HEART

- Why do you think God wanted Solomon to build the Temple rather than David?

- Have you experienced something similar to David here? How did you handle being told "no"?

- How do we find the balance between seeking God's will and timing versus overly analyzing everything but doing nothing?

DAY 11

1 KINGS: MAKE UP YOUR MIND
READING: 1 KINGS 18.

FOCUS: *So Ahab sent to all the people of Israel and gathered the prophets together at Mount Carmel. And Elijah came near to all the people and said, "How long will you go limping between two different opinions? If the LORD is God, follow him; but if Baal, then follow him." And the people did not answer him a word. Then Elijah said to the people, "I, even I only, am left a prophet of the LORD, but Baal's prophets are 450 men. Let two bulls be given to us, and let them choose one bull for themselves and cut it in pieces and lay it on the wood, but put no fire to it. And I will prepare the other bull and lay it on the wood and put no fire to it. And you call upon the name of your god, and I will call upon the name of the LORD, and the God who answers by fire, he is God." And all the people answered, "It is well spoken."*

1 Kings 18:20-24

Somewhere in the world on a certain day in history, someone decided to attempt the mixing of chocolate and peanut butter. Probably a different person at a different time dipped a cookie into milk for the first time, and history was made. To these unknown heroes, we owe a debt of gratitude for the discovery of things that mix together with glorious results. However, others have ruined perfectly good foods by adding unnecessary and truly uncalled-for ingredients. For example, ketchup is an appropriate condiment for French fries but certainly not for steak. Furthermore, under no circumstances should ketchup ever be put on tamales. (Remember, just say no.)

In Elijah's day, the people of Israel had no intention of completely walking away from Yahweh. After all, they were not opposed to receiving His help. The problem was that they wanted to worship and serve God but also worship Baal and his supposed consort Asherah. They wanted a mixture. Maybe they simply wanted to cover all the bases – just in case they were missing out on something. Sadly, the modern person often assumes that picking and choosing the more appealing parts of any and every religion and mixing them all together into a faith of one's own choosing is a recent development. However, affirming something doesn't make the idea true – anymore than denial automatically makes something untrue.

God knows Who He is. Consequently, He will not share His rightful place as God with anyone or anything else, especially the gods of man's invention that exist only in his warped imagination. Like many people today, the people of Israel wanted God but only on their terms and alongside their other gods. But God was having none of it. Baal was supposedly the god of fertility who provided the rains so that the land would produce food. Yet since no rain had fallen in three years before Elijah's challenge, Elijah saw the opportunity to call out the false gods and their prophets in the sight of all the people.

Notice that Elijah doesn't beg the people to follow the Lord. He doesn't lay out a proposal with all the benefits of serving God and the disadvantages of Baal worship. After Elijah pointed out that the people no longer could continue to be on the fence, his challenge was direct and rather simple: "If the LORD is God, follow Him; but if Baal, then follow him." Both/and was not an option – this decision was an either/or.

When Elijah suggested a "showdown" between Yahweh and the false gods, even the dense people of Israel must have recognized that the time had come to decide. Now, before we decide to start calling down fire from heaven on something (or some*one*), let's keep in mind that Elijah had been directed clearly by the Lord to do what he was about to do. We should not expect God to jump through any hoops because we want to prove someone wrong. On that day, however, God was going to make Himself known. Sometimes God speaks loudly and dramatically, and other times His whisper is heard only by those who are listening intently. (1 Kings 19:12)

The prophets of Baal did all they knew to do. They set up the altar and sacrifice; and they cried out, "O Baal, answer us!" But no fire fell — not even a spark. After this continued and the Baal worshipers grew more desperate, Elijah began to enjoy the pathetic spectacle. "And at noon Elijah mocked them, saying, 'Cry aloud, for he is a god. Either he is musing, or he is relieving himself, or he is on a journey, or perhaps he is asleep and must be awakened'" (1 Kings 18:27). Can't you just see Elijah walking up to the altar and pretending to warm his hands by the nonexistent "fire"?

When the fire fell from Heaven and consumed Elijah's sacrifice and everything around it, the people fell on their faces and said, "The Lord, He is God! The Lord, He is God!" But He always had been. In His mercy, Yahweh was making Himself known and demonstrating the foolishness of Baal worship. Elijah had prayed that God would turn back the hearts of His people that they would know that He alone is God. Perhaps we will not see His fire fall in the same way, but we can be assured that our false gods will fail us.

We might smugly argue that we would not be so foolish as to worship Baal the fertility god, but we nonetheless have gods of our own making. Are we chasing after money, success, power or longevity? Are there good things that we turn into idols when we desire His blessings more than His presence? Elijah's words still speak powerfully to us today. If our idols are worthy of our worship, then we should give ourselves to pursuing them. But if God really is God, then let's follow Him.

HEAD TO HEART

- In what ways have you seen your false gods fail you? What life pursuits have left you empty and disappointed?

- Do you think the Gospel should be presented as a plea to "please come and follow Jesus" or more of a challenge to trust in the true and Living God?

- Why doesn't God do things like send fire from Heaven more often? Would that help people believe?

DAY 12

2 KINGS: DON'T YOU KNOW I'M IMPORTANT?

READING: 2 KINGS 5.

FOCUS: *So Naaman came with his horses and chariots and stood at the door of Elisha's house. And Elisha sent a messenger to him, saying, "Go and wash in the Jordan seven times, and your flesh shall be restored, and you shall be clean." But Naaman was angry and went away, saying, "Behold, I thought that he would surely come out to me and stand and call upon the name of the LORD his God, and wave his hand over the place and cure the leper. Are not Abana and Pharpar, the rivers of Damascus, better than all the waters of Israel? Could I not wash in them and be clean?" So he turned and went away in a rage. But his servants came near and said to him, "My father, it is a great word the prophet has spoken to you; will you not do it? Has he actually said to you, 'Wash, and be clean'?" So he went down and dipped himself seven times in the Jordan, according to the word of the man of God, and his flesh was restored like the flesh of a little child, and he was clean.*

2 Kings 5:9-14

Naaman was a really important man. Don't believe it? Just ask him. The dilemma for Naaman was the increasing challenge of being really important but also having leprosy. He had won battles as the commander of the Syrian army and was a mighty man of valor, but his condition was worsening to the point of desperation.

The saving grace for Naaman was that a servant girl in his household didn't bear a grudge. The Israelite girl who had been captured and removed from her family in a Syrian raid could have remained silent as Naaman's affliction increased. After all, maybe the leprosy was God's retaliation for how she had been treated. But she knew about Elisha and God's power to heal through the prophet. Naaman was apparently desperate enough to ask for help — even help from a lowly Israelite.

In Naaman's mind, Elisha was being bestowed the great honor of the opportunity to help such an important person like himself. Since people tend to form expectations of others based on self-importance, Naaman likely assumed that Elisha already was rolling out the red carpet in anticipation of his arrival. It wasn't every day that Elisha had the chance to heal a man as important as Naaman.

But when Naaman and his entourage arrived, Elisha didn't even come to the door, forfeiting his opportunity to be in the presence of greatness and treating Naaman as though he were a door-to-door salesman. The doctor would not see him now. The mighty man of valor only got a messenger with a prescription. To add insult to injury, Naaman thought the prescription was ridiculous and far beneath a man of his importance. Important people apparently don't dunk themselves, especially not seven times. Besides, if he simply needed a bath, he could have stayed in Syria. "Behold, I thought that he would surely come out to me and stand and call upon the name of the LORD his God, and wave his hand over the place and cure the leper. Are not Abana and Pharpar, the rivers of Damascus, better than all the waters of Israel? Could I not wash in them and be clean?" Elisha had failed to appreciate that Naaman was *important*, but evidently lepers can't be choosers.

Again, Naaman is saved by his servants. They pointed out that he would have been willing to follow Elisha's directions if he deemed the instructions worthy of a man of his stature. But since the instructions were profoundly simple (and because he was in such a bad predicament), shouldn't he simply do as instructed? Elisha had not refused to help him, but Naaman did not appreciate the *way* he was helping. Of all people, however, the servants could advise Naaman here. Who would better understand doing a seemingly menial task?

Thankfully, Naaman was either wise or desperate enough to follow directions. More than likely, he felt silly after the third or fourth dip under the water and muttered unrepeatable things under his breath.

The only thing that happened the first six times is that Naaman got wet; but after the seventh time under the water, Naaman came out clean and restored. Evidently, he came away from the whole experience with a measure of humility also. "Then he returned to the man of God, he and all his company, and he came and stood before him. And he said, 'Behold, I know that there is no God in all the earth but in Israel; so accept now a present from your servant'" (2 Kings 5:15).

Often we are more like Naaman than we would want to believe. While we hopefully are not afflicted with leprosy, Naaman's haughty attitude and reluctant obedience resemble our own. We want to define the terms of our obedience. We get offended by God's direction because many times obedience involves humbling ourselves. But if we can supposedly do great things for God, why can't we do the small things?

We often wait for God to ask us to do something big and glamorous, but isn't it interesting that no one feels "called" to smaller tasks or assignments? We might argue, "But God, I really wanted to do something important!" Most of the time, we just wanted to be important. Are you too good to do something small? Will you persevere in obeying Him when the results aren't immediately seen? Although he almost walked away in a huff, Naaman was certainly glad he swallowed his pride and obeyed. May we do the same.

HEAD TO HEART

- In what ways has your pride or self-importance hindered you from obeying the Lord?

- Is there any area of your life in which you haven't obeyed God *completely?*

- How have your story and what God has done in your life been a blessing to others?

DAY 13

1 CHRONICLES: SIGNIFICANCE IN INSIGNIFICANCE

READING: 1 CHRONICLES 1.

FOCUS: *Adam, Seth, Enosh; Kenan, Mahalalel, Jared; Enoch, Methuselah, Lamech; Noah, Shem, Ham, and Japheth. The sons of Japheth: Gomer, Magog, Madai, Javan, Tubal, Meshech, and Tiras. The sons of Gomer: Ashkenaz, Riphath, and Togarmah. The sons of Javan: Elishah, Tarshish, Kittim, and Rodanim.*

The sons of Ham: Cush, Egypt, Put, and Canaan. The sons of Cush: Seba, Havilah, Sabta, Raamah, and Sabteca. The sons of Raamah: Sheba and Dedan. Cush fathered Nimrod. He was the first on earth to be a mighty man. Egypt fathered Ludim, Anamim, Lehabim, Naphtuhim, Pathrusim, Casluhim (from whom the Philistines came), and Caphtorim.

1 Chronicles 1:1-12

Upon reading a fascinating genealogical section of Scripture like this one, you might find yourself continually asking the question, "Why?" If you aren't asking that question from today's reading, just keep reading in 1 Chronicles as the lists of names continue for the first nine chapters! You would not be the first nor will you be the last to notice that this is not the most inspirational reading. And yet, out of all the things that the Holy Spirit could have included in the Bible, He led the Chronicler to include these lists.

Maybe you are not entirely fascinated by the sons of Gomer or Tavan. You probably could think of things that interest you more than Lehabim, Naphtuhim or even Pathrusim. After all, they lived and died a long time ago; and now they are just names on a page — even if that page is included in the Bible. So what do we do with such passages? For most people, their solution is to avoid them. These sections are not as interesting or helpful as others, so they typically are skipped. But was God's intention for us to neglect large sections of His Word? Does any passage of Scripture derive its value from how much it appeals to or inspires us? Surely, there is more to consider. Still, even an avid Bible reader often skims — rather than carefully reads — such portions. What can be gleaned from names, names and more names?

Perhaps the greatest value in such long genealogies is not so much in reading or memorizing each and every name but in considering all of the names as a whole. For example, thousands upon thousands of visitors travel to Washington, D.C. to view a long granite wall with nothing but a list of names. Why would that attract a crowd? The majority of visitors might recognize only a name or two out of the more than 58,000 names etched on the wall. Why visit a place to read names of people that you have never met?

For those who have been to the Vietnam Veterans Memorial, they know that the long list of names is much more than a long list of names. Almost no one starts at the beginning and reads every single name, but the entire monument provides a somber and powerful experience. Beyond knowing the commonality of those who lost their lives fighting a war in Vietnam, visitors know that every name on the wall represents a life – a son or a daughter, a husband or a wife, a father or a mother whose life and death were important to someone. And to God.

The people in the lists of names in the Bible may or may not have died in a war; but as we come to such sections of Scripture, we can take a similar approach as we might to a memorial. Although we know not a single person in the list of names, we know that every name (even the ones we can't pronounce) represents a life, a person who God created and loved — each with a story. If we allow them, their lives remind us of God's faithfulness to His people in ages past. Be encouraged by the thought that God has been present and active in the lives of His people thousands of years before you ever existed. His faithfulness did not begin and will not end with us. Truly history is "His-story."

Lists of names are also humbling. Even as we often fight the temptation to see ourselves as the center of the universe, we are struck with the reality that our name is merely one of many on a list that will be completely unknown soon after we are dead and gone. Sometimes we do well to be overwhelmed with our own insignificance. Someday your name may be listed alongside many obscure others such as Ashkenaz, Riphath and Togarmah. Someone may read your name with as much interest as you have for Sabteca. That's rather humbling.

The point of our lives has never been about making our name great or achieving a temporary fame. People have been trying and failing ever since the Tower of Babel. (Genesis 11) What we can do is make the most of the days we are granted and live today with a focus towards what will matter eternally. In the span of history, we are humbled to know that we are all just names on a wall. But that being the case, you can be astonished to know that God Himself knows *you* by name.

HEAD TO HEART

- If you have ever walked around in a cemetery and read the names and dates on the graves, what were your thoughts and ponderings?

- Besides what we have considered, what other reasons might God have for including the "less inspirational" sections of His Word?

- If someone were to read about your life long after you are dead, what would you want to be said about you?

DAY 14

2 CHRONICLES: FALLING AT THE FINISH LINE

READING: 2 CHRONICLES 14-16.

FOCUS: *In the thirty-ninth year of his reign Asa was diseased in his feet, and his disease became severe. Yet even in his disease he did not seek the LORD, but sought help from physicians. And Asa slept with his fathers, dying in the forty-first year of his reign. They buried him in the tomb that he had cut for himself in the city of David. They laid him on a bier that had been filled with various kinds of spices prepared by the perfumer's art, and they made a very great fire in his honor.*

2 Chronicles 16:12-14

Many have daydreamed about running in the Olympics or some other race and lunging across the finish line to win the race as the imaginary crowd goes wild. However, probably no one imagines running a great race but suddenly tripping and falling on their face just short of the finish line. Not everyone who has run a great race also has been able to finish well. Snatching defeat from the jaws of victory is easier than we might imagine.

King Asa of Judah overall was a good king. Considering the times in which he lived and the duration of his reign (41 years), Asa was exceptional. After the kingdom of Israel had split into the northern kingdom of Israel and the southern kingdom of Judah (1 Kings 12) and after the two forgettable kings before him, Asa provided Judah with much needed stability and leadership. Meanwhile the kingship in Israel was a revolving door as succession often was brought about by murder.

"And Asa did what was good and right in the eyes of the LORD his God" (2 Chronicles 14:2). He could not have asked for a more favorable description, and Judah could not have asked for a better leader. Asa even removed his own mother from power because of her idolatry, and the Chronicler added that "the heart of Asa was wholly true all his days" (2 Chronicles 15:17). When Judah was being threatened by a powerful, numerous enemy, Asa trusted the Lord. Listen to his words as he prayed: "O LORD, there is none like you to help, between the mighty and the weak. Help us, O LORD our God, for we rely on you, and in your name we have come against this multitude. O LORD, you are our God; let not man prevail against you" (2 Chronicles 14:11). When God gave them victory, Asa and the army of Judah ended up plundering those who once had been so threatening. Asa trusted God, and God demonstrated that He is trustworthy.

Yes, Asa was a great king and a great man – at least until he inexplicably stopped trusting God. Having trusted the Lord before and having seen God deliver a great victory over a much bigger threat, Asa did not trust the Lord fully when he was threatened by Baasha, the king of Israel. We might wonder if Asa had the expectation that, since he had served faithfully for so long, he then was entitled to no further difficulties. Maybe Asa was angry that the Lord had allowed this situation; but whatever the case, he turned to Syria instead of trusting the Lord. Even worse, Asa used silver and gold from the Temple to pay the king of Syria for his assistance.

On a surface level, the strategy was effective. The threat from the king of Israel was removed, so problem solved! But Asa had acted foolishly, and the matter would not be swept under the royal rug. Hanani the seer confronted Asa and pointed out how Asa had failed to trust the Lord — even though God had rescued Judah against more formidable foes in the past. "For the eyes of the LORD run to and fro throughout the whole earth, to give strong support to those whose heart is blameless toward him. You have done foolishly in this, for from now on you will have wars" (2 Chronicles 16:9).

Hanani's words should have humbled Asa, but instead Asa flew into a rage and had Hanani imprisoned. Asa was angry because he knew he was wrong. He even took out his anger on the people of Judah. After such a long and effective tenure, Asa crashed and burned. Perhaps this was the last hurdle in the race, but Asa stumbled and tumbled, never getting back up or returning to his previous form.

Even when he became severely afflicted, Asa refused to turn back to the Lord. On other occasions, God would respond with grace towards the humble — even from wicked kings (2 Chronicles 33:19); but Asa remained obstinate in his affliction. After a long tenure as king, Asa died from the disease and without seeking the Lord.

What happened to Asa? We are left to wonder why Asa seemingly got tired of relying on the Lord. Maybe the success went to his head. Maybe he wanted to take more credit than what was really due. Whatever the case, Asa wouldn't be the last one to finish badly. No matter our successes or failures, we never reach the point where we are not utterly dependent on the Lord. We may be seasoned, mature believers; but we never reach the point that we are immune from falling. May each of us walk humbly and depend on His grace to finish well.

Hebrews 12:1-2 says, "Therefore, since we are surrounded by so great a cloud of witnesses, let us also lay aside every weight, and sin which clings so closely, and let us run with endurance the race that is set before us, looking to Jesus, the founder and perfecter of our faith, who for the joy that was set before him endured the cross, despising the shame, and is seated at the right hand of the throne of God."

HEAD TO HEART

- In what ways have you trusted the Lord in the past and seen Him bring you through a trial?

- What do you think happened to Asa to cause him to stop trusting and relying on the Lord after doing so well for so long?

- What safeguards can you establish in your life in the effort to finish your race well?

DAY 15

EZRA: THE KINGS AND THE KING
READING: EZRA 1; 2 CHRONICLES 36:17-23.

FOCUS: *In the first year of Cyrus king of Persia, that the word of the LORD by the mouth of Jeremiah might be fulfilled, the LORD stirred up the spirit of Cyrus king of Persia, so that he made a proclamation throughout all his kingdom and also put it in writing: "Thus says Cyrus king of Persia: The LORD, the God of heaven, has given me all the kingdoms of the earth, and he has charged me to build him a house at Jerusalem, which is in Judah. Whoever is among you of all his people, may his God be with him, and let him go up to Jerusalem, which is in Judah, and rebuild the house of the LORD, the God of Israel—he is the God who is in Jerusalem. And let each survivor, in whatever place he sojourns, be assisted by the men of his place with silver and gold, with goods and with beasts, besides freewill offerings for the house of God that is in Jerusalem." Then rose up the heads of the fathers' houses of Judah and Benjamin, and the priests and the Levites, everyone whose spirit God had stirred to go up to rebuild the house of the LORD that is in Jerusalem.*

Ezra 1:1-5

"The king's heart is a stream of water in the hand of the LORD; he turns it wherever he will."

Proverbs 21:1

The rulers of this world possess power for an appointed season, but Jesus has all authority in heaven and on earth. (Matthew 28:19) Kingdoms rise and fall, empires come and go and kings are here today, gone tomorrow as history marches on to the day when "The kingdom of the world has become the kingdom of our Lord and of his Christ, and he shall reign forever and ever" (Revelation 11:15).

We don't know the exact nature of King Cyrus' relationship with the

Lord, but what history and archaeology have revealed wouldn't suggest that Cyrus was a full-on follower of Yahweh. Although he was likely the most powerful person in the world at that time, Cyrus seemed to understand that God had given him an assignment and that the kingdoms of the world truly had been given to him by God. Not only did Cyrus allow the people of Judah to return to Jerusalem to rebuild, he even sent them with his blessing. After decades of Jerusalem and the Temple sitting in ruins, the long process of rebuilding would begin.

But why would a Persian king care if there was a Temple in Jerusalem? Since the Temple had been destroyed by the Babylonians 70 years before, why would it make any difference to Cyrus that the Temple would be rebuilt? In an earthly sense, the plight of the exiles from Judah and the restoration of their Temple were not Cyrus' problem; but this is exactly why his actions are so remarkable. The only explanation is that God can move the heart of a king to do His will and accomplish His purpose.

Did God orchestrate events so that the right king would be in position when the right time came? Or was the king himself insignificant because God would direct the heart of the king regardless of the man? We don't truly know the answer, but what we do know is that God worked in fulfillment of His promise. The decision that Cyrus believed was his to make had been decreed by God before the Persian Empire existed and before King Cyrus was born.

Long before Jeremiah had spoken these words: "This whole land shall become a ruin and a waste, and these nations shall serve the king of Babylon seventy years. Then after seventy years are completed, I will punish the king of Babylon and that nation, the land of the Chaldeans, for their iniquity, declares the LORD, making the land an everlasting waste. I will bring upon that land all the words that I have uttered against it, everything written in this book, which Jeremiah prophesied against all the nations. For many nations and great kings shall make slaves even of them, and I will recompense them according to their deeds and the work of their hands" (Jeremiah 25:11-14).

Cyrus made the decree because God already had decreed what would happen. The 70 years were up, and the Babylonians had been taken down. Concerning His people, God had said, "Behold, I will gather them from all the countries to which I drove them in my anger and my wrath and in great indignation. I will bring them back to this place, and I will make them dwell in safety. And they shall be my people, and I will be their God" (Jeremiah 32:37-38).

The road to Jerusalem was long, and the rebuilding process was even longer. Difficult days were now behind the exiles, but many more were still ahead. Yet God fulfilled His promise when He moved the heart of the king.

Today you may not like the direction in which things seem to be headed in your nation. You may not believe that the right people are in the right positions in your government. You may not see how God is working as the events of the day unfold. But God hasn't surrendered His authority. His will *will* be done in heaven *and* on earth. Earthly rulers and governments may seem to be in opposition to His ultimate rule, but they can do nothing outside of what He allows. Once an Egyptian ruler tried to resist His will, but Pharaoh learned Who truly rules the world. (Exodus 1-14) Others have tried with the same result. Pray for those who are (currently) in authority, knowing that He has all authority.

HEAD TO HEART

- Why would God use godless rulers to do His will instead of establishing Godly rulers who would *want* to do His will?

- What should our attitude be towards authorities who operate in opposition to God's Word?

- Do you pray for those who are currently in authority or spend more time complaining about them?

DAY 16

NEHEMIAH: THE TOOLS OF OPPOSITION
READING: NEHEMIAH 4.

FOCUS: *Now when Sanballat heard that we were building the wall, he was angry and greatly enraged, and he jeered at the Jews. And he said in the presence of his brothers and of the army of Samaria, "What are these feeble Jews doing? Will they restore it for themselves? Will they sacrifice? Will they finish up in a day? Will they revive the stones out of the heaps of rubbish, and burned ones at that?" Tobiah the Ammonite was beside him, and he said, "Yes, what they are building—if a fox goes up on it he will break down their stone wall!" Hear, O our God, for we are despised. Turn back their taunt on their own heads and give them up to be plundered in a land where they are captives. Do not cover their guilt, and let not their sin be blotted out from your sight, for they have provoked you to anger in the presence of the builders. So we built the wall. And all the wall was joined together to half its height, for the people had a mind to work.*

Nehemiah 4:1-6

When we set out to do the Lord's work, we often naively assume that the work will go smoothly, that the results will be tremendous and that our efforts will be appreciated. This optimism lasts at least until we actually start doing the work. Then we often discover the work is challenging, seemingly accomplishes very little and that people are unappreciative — if not outright critical.

When King Cyrus decreed that the Jews could return to Jerusalem after the Exile and begin the process of rebuilding the city and the Temple (Ezra 1), no one had likely expected that the process would take so long and be so difficult. Decades had passed, and the work still hadn't been completed. Just as God had moved the heart of King Cyrus previously,

God granted Nehemiah an amazing degree of favor with Artaxerxes, the king of Persia, and Nehemiah was granted permission to go to Jerusalem to continue the work of restoration. (Nehemiah 1-2)

When Nehemiah arrived in Jerusalem, he saw the devastation both of what had been destroyed by the Babylonians originally as well as what had been rebuilt — only to be destroyed again. With all that remained to be done, Nehemiah would have appreciated a measure of progress. But in all the work of rebuilding, opposition came in abundance — primarily through the villain Sanballat.

Wasn't it enough that Nehemiah was doing the Lord's work? That being the case, shouldn't God have removed the obstacles and hindrances so that His work would be completed? After all, God already had removed significant obstacles for the work to begin and later for the work to resume. Why not remove every obstacle, especially the human ones, so the work could be completed? We might be inclined to think this way, but God rarely operates according to our expectations. God has His reasons.

Since Sanballat died thousands of years ago, you have never met him; but if his words and actions remind you of someone today, maybe they're distant cousins. If a particular person doesn't come to mind, we will recognize that our spiritual enemy still utilizes the same tactics of belittling, discouraging and accusing in opposition to the work that God is doing in and through us. After all, Sanballat learned those tactics somewhere, and the source is the same for the Sanballats we encounter today. You've likely heard some of the same questions, but they really aren't questions as much as accusations. "Why are you even doing this? Don't you know you're going to fail? Why would you think God could use you? Don't you remember what happened last time?"

But God allowed the opposition to exist and to continue. As a result, the work took much longer. Nehemiah had to divide up the work force so that half built the wall while the other half stood guard. (Nehemiah 4:15-20) Just think how much faster the wall could have been completed if half the workforce didn't have to stand guard all the time. Because of the opposition they faced, their attention was divided, but the work of rebuilding continued — even if the process was slow.

Without opposition, they might have built the wall faster but never learned to trust and rely on God in the process. Sure, God wanted the wall to be built; but He wanted the builders to trust in Him and not in what they were building. Walls were necessary for the defense of a city, but God wanted them to know that He was their Shield and Defender.

One of the amazing things about God is that He has everything at His disposal to continually refine us into His image. He can use our Godly friends; but He also can use our godless, heartless enemies. He can even use the schemes of our ultimate enemy to work for our good and His glory. If we don't seem to be shielded from opposition, we then can know that God will use that opposition. The Sanballats, who we suffer and endure today, are tools in God's hands — even if they can't recall volunteering for the role.

We can use the weapons that He has given us, especially the Word of God, to come against all of the distractions and discouragement the enemy tries to bring. God sometimes will allow the enemy to bring resistance to teach us how to resist the enemy and to trust Him more. The walls will get built in His timing; the work will be done in His way; and through the process, you will learn to trust Him more deeply.

HEAD TO HEART

- How have you typically responded to the Sanballats in your life? Fighting back? Appeasement?

- In what ways have you seen God be your Shield and Defender as you trusted Him in a particular situation?

- Who has God used in your life to refine you that you did not consider to be a friend?

DAY 17

ESTHER: WHEN BITTERNESS TAKES HOLD
READING: ESTHER 5.

FOCUS: *And Haman went out that day joyful and glad of heart. But when Haman saw Mordecai in the king's gate, that he neither rose nor trembled before him, he was filled with wrath against Mordecai. Nevertheless, Haman restrained himself and went home, and he sent and brought his friends and his wife Zeresh. And Haman recounted to them the splendor of his riches, the number of his sons, all the promotions with which the king had honored him, and how he had advanced him above the officials and the servants of the king. Then Haman said, "Even Queen Esther let no one but me come with the king to the feast she prepared. And tomorrow also I am invited by her together with the king. Yet all this is worth nothing to me, so long as I see Mordecai the Jew sitting at the king's gate." Then his wife Zeresh and all his friends said to him, "Let a gallows fifty cubits high be made, and in the morning tell the king to have Mordecai hanged upon it. Then go joyfully with the king to the feast." This idea pleased Haman, and he had the gallows made.*

Esther 5:9-14

The Bible includes an abundance of characters — real men and women who loved God deeply but also failed miserably. We can learn from both the victories and struggles of God's people. But when we come to the book of Esther, we encounter Haman, one of the most diabolical people in all the Bible. You may remember that the book of Esther makes no explicit mention of God at all, yet we see His hand orchestrating the events of the story to rescue His people once again. The evil Haman could have been the poster child for spite and petty jealousy; but once again, what man intended for evil, God turned into good and the salvation of many.

If we could say anything positive about Haman, his evil heart was something that he may have "come by honestly" as the expression goes. Beyond the depravity into which all of us were born, the Bible mentions five different times that Haman was an Agagite. Many years before, King Saul disobeyed the command of the Lord to destroy the Amalekites whose king was Agag. (1 Samuel 15) While we don't know this for certain, Haman could have been a descendant of the Amalekites (or Agagites) who had been enemies of God's people since the days of Moses.

Is there anyone who almost immediately can alter your mood? Hopefully, there are people who can change your mood for the better; but you likely know a few people who can cast a dark shadow over just about anything. Your day is ruined at the sight of them. In the same way, one day Haman was so joyful that he practically was skipping – until he saw Mordecai who was a relative of Esther's. He essentially had raised Esther after she was orphaned. Additionally, Mordecai previously had overheard and foiled a plot to assassinate the king. For all that was good about Mordecai, Haman nevertheless loathed him.

With a name like Haman, we might wonder if Mordecai perhaps had annoyed him by saying, "Hey man!" every time he saw him; but that only would be speculation. No, the real reason Haman hated Mordecai was that Mordecai would not bow to him. Even worse, Mordecai was not afraid of Haman; and this reality was eating Haman alive. Haman could not enjoy the favor he was receiving and all the things that were going well for him as long as there was one Jewish guy who refused to pay him homage. But Haman hardly would be the last person to allow bitterness over a perceived slight to dominate his emotions and outlook. As we read about Haman and Mordecai, the pettiness and childishness of Haman are perceived easily. Perhaps we aren't expecting others to bow before us; but once we feel insulted, disregarded or even ignored by someone else, we can approach that same level of bitterness.

Haman's solution was simple but also a bit drastic. Mordecai should die for such a heinous offense — at least as Haman saw things, and the gallows were prepared. This seems extreme because, of course, it was; but is there anyone we might like to see destroyed? Not that we plan to send anyone to the gallows personally, but would we inwardly rejoice if they got what we hope is coming to them?

What Haman failed to realize is that God was quietly orchestrating events to preserve His people — even as Haman was actively plotting and scheming to eliminate not only Mordecai but all of God's people. Perhaps had Haman been able to let go of his personal vendetta against Mordecai, he also would have not pushed to annihilate all the Jews. When Queen Esther revealed her Jewish ethnicity and exposed Haman as the one behind the extermination plot, the King was enraged. Haman then was executed on the same gallows he had prepared for Mordecai. Irony can be wonderful.

We cheer the happy outcome and God's hand in what took place, but we also do well to consider Haman's raging bitterness as well as our own. The wrongs done to us likely have not been petty or small. Living in a fallen and broken world, we likely have been legitimately hurt. Our expectations were not that another person bow down to us, but we did expect them to at least treat us with respect and dignity. And yet they didn't. We would like to think that we never could be as spiteful and vindictive as Haman, but bitterness truly is poison. Learn from Haman. *Destroy bitterness or bitterness eventually will destroy you.* Having been completely forgiven in Christ, we in turn show grace to those who deserve grace the least.

HEAD TO HEART

- Are you harboring bitterness or resentment towards anyone? If or when you have, how is your relationship with God or others affected?

- How do you typically respond when you feel slighted or disregarded by another person?

- How do you forgive someone when they have not apologized nor sought your forgiveness?

DAY 18

JOB: WHEN THE SKY IS FALLING

READING: JOB 1-2.

FOCUS: *Now there was a day when the sons of God came to present themselves before the LORD, and Satan also came among them. The LORD said to Satan, "From where have you come?" Satan answered the LORD and said, "From going to and fro on the earth, and from walking up and down on it." And the LORD said to Satan, "Have you considered my servant Job, that there is none like him on the earth, a blameless and upright man, who fears God and turns away from evil?" Then Satan answered the LORD and said, "Does Job fear God for no reason? Have you not put a hedge around him and his house and all that he has, on every side? You have blessed the work of his hands, and his possessions have increased in the land. But stretch out your hand and touch all that he has, and he will curse you to your face." And the LORD said to Satan, "Behold, all that he has is in your hand. Only against him do not stretch out your hand." So Satan went out from the presence of the LORD.*

Job 1:6-12

Again there was a day when the sons of God came to present themselves before the LORD, and Satan also came among them to present himself before the LORD. And the LORD said to Satan, "From where have you come?" Satan answered the LORD and said, "From going to and fro on the earth, and from walking up and down on it." And the LORD said to Satan, "Have you considered my servant Job, that there is none like him on the earth, a blameless and upright man, who fears God and turns away from evil? He still holds fast his integrity, although you incited me against him to destroy him without reason." Then Satan answered the LORD and said, "Skin for skin! All that a man has he will give for his life. But stretch out your hand and touch his bone and his flesh, and he will curse you to your face." And the LORD said to Satan, "Behold, he is in your hand; only spare his life."

Job 2:1-6

Some of us give way too much time and energy to worrying about the worst-case scenario actually happening, but no amount of worry will help. However, sometimes the worst-case scenario does, in fact, happen or at least something just as bad that we didn't anticipate. Had we known, we could have worried in advance! Worrying about potential tragedies doesn't prevent them, but being naïve about life in a fallen world leaves a person woefully unprepared when tragedy strikes. Just as the tallest tree in the forest will be the one that lightning strikes, Godly people are not exempt from tragedies but likely will endure suffering to an even greater degree.

Job was a good man, "blameless and upright, one who feared God and turned away from evil." By the way Job lived, he could have been the shining example for legalism: be good, obey the rules and watch how God will bless you! Ironically, Job also would have been the perfect example for the prosperity preachers: God wants you to be wealthy just like Job! (So send your donation now.) But shallow or false theology has neither room nor answer for the events that began to unfold in Job's life. The Holy Spirit inspired the Scriptures in such a way that we can read about the conversations taking place in the spiritual realm, but remember Job had no idea. We know what Job didn't, and that information is instructive for us today.

When all hell began to break loose around Job, he had no idea that Satan (literally, "the accuser") had approached God and said that Job was blameless only because God had made life so easy for him. When Job's property was destroyed, his possessions stolen and his children killed, Job obviously was devastated but did not know why these things were happening. When Job's body was tormented with pain, he knew enough to accept affliction from God, but he still didn't know the cause or the purpose.

But we know that God gave Satan permission to afflict Job. That can be a troubling thought but also one that offers glorious encouragement. We might initially question why God would allow Satan to do such things. Why not tell Satan to take a hike and leave His servants alone? Why not ignore Satan's accusations since God truly knew Job's heart? Job's experiences and the inclusion of his story in the Bible invite us to wrestle with difficult questions about life but, more specifically, difficult questions about God and His ways.

But notice a few things. Satan did not have free rein to torment Job; he first needed God's approval. In both conversations, God set limits and specific parameters on what Satan could do and not do. In other words, God was calling the shots and making all of the rules. Satan was and still is under God's authority. The enemy could do nothing to Job that God had not allowed him to do. God used Satan. Even as Satan might have thought he would embarrass God, the whole conspiracy backfired. Yes, Job suffered greatly and would struggle to understand what God was doing. Meanwhile, Job's so-called friends foolishly argued that his suffering was the direct result of sin. And when God at last responded to Job's direct questions, the answer Job received was essentially that He is God, and we are not. (Job 38-42)

Whether you tend to worry or not, know this: God has Satan on a leash. The enemy can do nothing to you that God doesn't allow, and whatever God permits in your life is for your good and His glory and proceeds out of His love for you. The suffering we have endured and will endure on the path of obedience is not the result of the enemy's schemes but of God's goodness. We will live and die with unanswered questions — perhaps the same questions that Job asked, but those things remain beyond our knowledge or comprehension. Job learned that since he could not answer all of God's questions, he also could not handle God's answers. He is still God, and we are still not.

But for today, knowing that God has a plan is enough. You are His child, a part of His purpose and made for His glory. Satan can't even look in your direction without God's permission, and whatever God might allow him to do in your life ultimately will be a blessing. The malicious intent of the enemy for your harm is gloriously overpowered by God's determination to cause all things to work together for your good. Today may be a tough season; but the trials you suffer are neither random nor pointless and are never, for a moment, out of His loving control.

HEAD TO HEART

- What is wrong with the assumption that living a good life results in prosperity and ease?

- How have you typically responded when your life isn't what you had expected or God gives you something you didn't want?

- How have you seen God use the enemy's evil plans for good in your life?

DAY 19

PSALMS: WHEN GOD IS TAKING TOO LONG

READING: PSALM 13.

FOCUS: *How long, O LORD? Will you forget me forever? How long will you hide your face from me? How long must I take counsel in my soul and have sorrow in my heart all the day? How long shall my enemy be exalted over me? Consider and answer me, O LORD my God; light up my eyes, lest I sleep the sleep of death, lest my enemy say, "I have prevailed over him," lest my foes rejoice because I am shaken. But I have trusted in your steadfast love; my heart shall rejoice in your salvation. I will sing to the LORD, because he has dealt bountifully with me.*

Psalm 13:1-6

"How long, O LORD? Will you forget me forever?" Now what could be more encouraging and uplifting than that? You may have asked those very questions while listening to a long-winded preacher! Unlike other Psalms, we are not told the circumstances in David's life that brought him to compose these words; but the way in which David deals with his circumstances gives us help in dealing with our trials and gives us a better understanding of God. While typically seen as a lament, Psalm 13 also brings us comforting news.

Whatever was taking place in David's life, we can discern a few things with certainty. First, the situation is beyond difficult. Each of us faces different challenges, and only the person facing them truly understands the degree of difficulty. Secondly, the trial has dragged on for a long time. As we mature in the faith, we come to expect trials; but we don't expect them to stay around. We want to endure the trial, learn the lesson and then move on. But sometimes the trial lingers, and there seems to be no point or lesson — just prolonged suffering.

Finally, to make David's situation worse, people were involved. David was pained to see his enemy exalted and cried out for God to intervene. As David was experiencing, certain people seemingly live to make us miserable. But sometimes even well-meaning, well-intentioned people seem to have a gift, a special flair for making things worse. People tend to assume they understand your situation and somehow know exactly what you should do. In reality, the best way they could help you is by not trying to help you.

But still all of this is good news. How? We first can be comforted to know that someone else has felt the way we're feeling. We are not alone in our misery. Rest assured that you are not the first one to be frustrated with God, to have doubts about God and to wish God would just do something. Knowing that others have felt that way at times doesn't make your situation go away, but we can be comforted knowing that "it's not just me." One of the tactics of the enemy is to make us feel completely alone both in our sin and in our suffering. This is yet another reason for reading the Bible, especially Psalms like this that give us words for our current situation.

Also, we can be comforted to know that we are allowed to express our frustration and disappointment — both to God and to each other. God is not threatened by your disappointment. He's not the least bit insecure. Jeremiah 12:1 says, "Righteous are you, O Lord, when I complain to you; yet I would plead my case before you. Why does the way of the wicked prosper? Why do all who are treacherous thrive?" Jeremiah knew God was in the right because God is always in the right, but he complained anyway because he knew that his complaint mattered to God.

Expressing our frustration to God is a recognition of His sovereignty and control over all that happens. We're acknowledging that what's happening or not happening to us isn't random and comes from the hand of God. If you have felt abandoned by God, this affirms your faith in God. You wouldn't feel abandoned if you truly believed there was never anyone there!

We also are allowed to express our frustration to each other. Not that we would share everything or share with everyone, but we need people in our lives with whom we can be open and honest. Your truest friends are the people to whom you don't have to explain yourself. As C. S. Lewis said, "Friendship is born at the moment when one man says to another, 'What? You too? I thought I was the only one.'"

David clearly was overwhelmed by his circumstances and acknowledged he was finished if God didn't come through. If David were around today, someone might even try to encourage David by spouting cliches like "God will never give you more than you can handle." Wrong. God indeed will give us way more than we can handle – but what He allows in our lives will never be more than He can handle.

God does put us in situations in which, if He does not lead us through the darkness, we will be lost. If He does not protect us, we'll be hurt or even killed. If He does not fight for us, we will be defeated. But that causes our eyes to look to Him and not to ourselves. We want to feel like we're in control, that we clearly see where we're going, that we're going to have victory by our own doing. God loves to rescue His people, but He uses our trials to rescue us from the illusion of our self-sufficiency. Eventually, He rescues us from the trial; but even now, He is rescuing us *through* the trial. Remember that God's perfect track record of faithfulness to His children will not end with you.

By the end of this brief Psalm, David has gone from asking aloud if God has forgotten him to celebrating God's love and favor. What changed between the first verse and the last verse? Probably nothing, at least circumstantially. What did change is David's perspective. He set his focus on God, and now God is bigger than the problem. The huge dilemma now pales in comparison to the goodness of God. We never know when or if things will get better, but we do know that God is bigger than whatever we will face.

HEAD TO HEART

- Are you in a "Psalm 13 season" right now? How does David's prayer encourage and guide you?

- How do you know when you are appropriately bringing your frustrations to God or simply griping?

- Who has inspired you by the way in which they have suffered and endured their trials?

DAY 20

PROVERBS: WISDOM WITH WORDS
READING: PROVERBS 15.

FOCUS: *A soft answer turns away wrath, but a harsh word stirs up anger.*

The tongue of the wise commends knowledge, but the mouths of fools pour out folly.

A gentle tongue is a tree of life, but perverseness in it breaks the spirit.

The lips of the wise spread knowledge; not so the hearts of fools.

To make an apt answer is a joy to a man, and a word in season, how good it is!

The heart of the righteous ponders how to answer, but the mouth of the wicked pours out evil things.

Proverbs 15:1-2, 4, 7, 23, 28

Hand, foot and mouth disease (HFMD) is a common and very contagious condition among infants and toddlers. The condition is spread because small children don't always have the best hygienic practices. Another condition, known as hoof-and-mouth disease, occurs among cows, sheep and pigs who also are apparently unfamiliar with best practices for disease prevention. Unrelated to either of these diseases is a common condition among all age groups of humans known as "Foot *in* Mouth" disease. Those who are suffering from Foot in Mouth do know better but afflict themselves and others anyway. This disease is not necessarily contagious, but it persists at alarming levels. While the entire population is vulnerable, certain people clearly are more prone to Foot in Mouth than others. A correlation exists between how much a person speaks and his or her susceptibility to this terrible sickness.

We're all guilty, aren't we? Whether we admit it or not, we have all put our foot in our mouth at one time or another. For some, the occurrences are rare and out of character. For others, we start to wonder if they didn't take lessons in saying the wrong thing. Sometimes the gaffe is comical, especially when a famous person or otherwise intelligent person spews something truly moronic. We enjoy a good laugh — provided we aren't the one who uttered the ridiculous. But other times, there's nothing amusing about saying the wrong thing.

Maybe the words sounded great in our head but not nearly as profound when the words came out of our mouths. Or the times when we knew what we were about to say only would escalate a bad situation, but we spoke the words anyway. We also may recall that morsel of gossip that was simply too good to not pass along, so we took the liberty to "share." And finally, too many times our anger got the best of us, resulting in vicious and critical words that were spoken to or about someone.

Saying the wrong thing comes so easily. Sometimes we may even say the right thing, but the timing is all wrong. A huge gap exists between someone speaking words that are life-giving and someone spewing their unsolicited (and often uninformed) opinion. Even when we might have something worthwhile to say, we demonstrate wisdom in being much slower to speak than we are to listen. We take something of a risk any time that we speak, especially when we are attempting to speak into a situation or a life.

Besides the untold effect that our words can have on others, the issue goes much deeper – all the way to the heart. Sometimes we misspeak or speak carelessly. We then immediately wish we could take back the words and give our mouths a mulligan. But more often, the problem lies in that we said exactly what we meant. We said what we said because, before the words ever came out of our mouths, they marinated within our hearts. Jesus said that "out of the abundance of the heart the mouth speaks" (Matthew 12:34). Our words are simply the overflow of our hearts. When sin comes out, the cause is the sin within.

But Proverbs and other Scriptures don't speak of our words in only negative terms. The tongue has tremendous potential to praise God and to bless others. In fact, death *and* life are in the power of the tongue. (Proverbs 18:21) Proverbs speaks continually about the pursuit and treasuring of wisdom. Biblical wisdom is not some intangible concept of some good ideas and deep thoughts. Wisdom is personified by the Holy Spirit. He teaches us and guides us into the truth.

When we are empowered by the Holy Spirit, we cannot only avoid speaking evil, but we have the ability to speak life and encouragement. The Spirit helps our words (and the discretion of our silence) to be "gracious, seasoned with salt, so that you may know how you ought to answer each person" (Colossians 4:6). The Bible speaks of an apt word or a word that is "fitly spoken." What a joy to hear the instruction, encouragement or even the correction of the words we needed to hear. What a privilege to speak words of life to someone else as the Spirit leads and empowers us. As much as you might remember hurtful words once spoken to you and perhaps still feel their sting, hopefully the life-giving and life-changing words someone spoke to you are even more resounding. May the Holy Spirit give each one of us wisdom in our words.

HEAD TO HEART

- What are the things you said that you regret the most? Have you been able to make amends?

- When you have said the wrong thing, what was driving or motivating your words?

- Who has spoken life and encouragement to you, and what impact did those words have in your heart?

DAY 21

ECCLESIASTES: THE ILLUSION OF CONTROL

READING: ECCLESIASTES 9.

FOCUS: *Again I saw that under the sun the race is not to the swift, nor the battle to the strong, nor bread to the wise, nor riches to the intelligent, nor favor to those with knowledge, but time and chance happen to them all. For man does not know his time. Like fish that are taken in an evil net, and like birds that are caught in a snare, so the children of man are snared at an evil time, when it suddenly falls upon them. I have also seen this example of wisdom under the sun, and it seemed great to me. There was a little city with few men in it, and a great king came against it and besieged it, building great siegeworks against it. But there was found in it a poor, wise man, and he by his wisdom delivered the city. Yet no one remembered that poor man. But I say that wisdom is better than might, though the poor man's wisdom is despised and his words are not heard. The words of the wise heard in quiet are better than the shouting of a ruler among fools. Wisdom is better than weapons of war, but one sinner destroys much good.*

Ecclesiastes 9:11-18

When you were in school, you probably either loved or loathed math; but at least the answers to the questions were predictable and precise. We may have had no idea how to get the answers, but at least there were answers. Your answer was right, or your answer was wrong. Even in a day when people are attempting to have their own "truth" and define reality according to their preferences, two plus two still equals four (so far). Maybe you were one who frequently asked when you'd need to use math in "real life." If nothing else, maybe math prepared you for life because both math and life are hard! But the difficulty of both may be the extent of what they have in common.

Have you noticed life isn't precise or predictable like math? Long before anyone claimed that death and taxes were the only certainties in life, the Preacher (the author of Ecclesiastes who was likely Solomon or at least one of his followers) noticed that time and chance happen to everyone. Life is both predictable and unpredictable. Sometimes the unexpected occurs; and other times, we can see what is going to happen well in advance.

If we've lived long enough, we know that this life cannot be reduced to simple or even complicated formulas because cause and effect doesn't always work in the way we anticipated. Hard work does not always pay off in the end – sometimes people labor and toil for nothing. We want our children to be inspired to make a huge impact on the world someday; but no, not everyone can be anything they want or dream to be. The prize doesn't always go to the most deserving. The most gifted doesn't always get noticed. The best team doesn't always win. Evil people prosper while good people suffer. Young people die in the prime of their lives, while others linger on long past the point at which they stopped living and are merely existing. The voice of wisdom goes unheard because the foolish voices speak louder and more often. The honorable are disregarded and ignored, while fools and their folly are celebrated.

The Preacher's observations were not the result of being in a foul mood but rather sober reflections from a thoughtful man who had experienced the good, the bad and the ugly of this life. Some will read his reflections and mutter something along the lines of "How depressing!" But others will quietly nod in affirmation because they have experienced the futility of this life for themselves. Many of us need no additional reminders that, for the time being, this is not heaven but earth. As much as we might want to be, we are not at all in control.

Perhaps you started out as a new Christian under the impression that living for Jesus would provide immunity from the brokenness of the world — only to discover that futility happens to you, too. No, following Jesus doesn't remove us from the realities of life described by the Preacher; but would you even want to think about navigating life without Him?

Ultimately, we are left with the choice between despair and hope. The Preacher concluded that all of life is vanity, a striving after the wind (Ecclesiastes 1:14), which is a realistic and wise perspective. Even Paul, who knew how to rejoice in the worst of afflictions, pointed out that all of creation has been subjected to futility. (Romans 8:20) Those things are true; and if that is where we stop, there is ample reason for despair.

But if we continue beyond the vanity and beyond the futility because of Jesus, there is hope. All that we experience in this life – the good, the bad, the profound and the utterly stupid – are merely preparation for the life that is to come. If you aren't experiencing all of the satisfaction and fulfillment you would like in your life today, you were not intended to have all of those things here. This is earth, not heaven. All of the things that continually remind us that we are not home yet can help us to anticipate, in hope, the time when "the creation itself will be set free from its bondage to corruption and obtain the freedom of the glory of the children of God" (Romans 8:21).

For the today that we have, trust God. Enjoy His blessings. Have no expectations that life in the here and now will be satisfying or even make sense. Put your hope in Jesus, and know the best is yet to come.

HEAD TO HEART

- What are some of the ways you see the futility or unfairness of this life?

- How do you typically respond when you experience these frustrations?

- How do you balance being realistic and yet hopeful about the life God has given to you?

DAY 22

SONG OF SOLOMON: GOD GIVES GOOD GIFTS

READING: SONG OF SOLOMON 4.

FOCUS: *Behold, you are beautiful, my love, behold, you are beautiful! Your eyes are doves behind your veil. Your hair is like a flock of goats leaping down the slopes of Gilead. Your teeth are like a flock of shorn ewes that have come up from the washing, all of which bear twins, and not one among them has lost its young. Your lips are like a scarlet thread, and your mouth is lovely. Your cheeks are like halves of a pomegranate behind your veil. Your neck is like the tower of David, built in rows of stone; on it hang a thousand shields, all of them shields of warriors. Your two breasts are like two fawns, twins of a gazelle, that graze among the lilies. Until the day breathes and the shadows flee, I will go away to the mountain of myrrh and the hill of frankincense. You are altogether beautiful, my love; there is no flaw in you.*

Song of Solomon 4:1-7

Unless you already are familiar with Song of Solomon (also called Song of Songs), you probably were surprised to find such a passage in the Bible. While telling someone that their hair is like a flock of goats or that their teeth are like a flock of sheep is not necessarily recommended as a pickup line today, this passage and others in Song of Solomon are romantic and, yes, sexual. As someone once said about this strange and surprising Old Testament book, "Well, Solomon had a lot to sing about." In fact, the language is so suggestive that some have assumed that the words must be allegorical and refer to intimacy with God. But Song of Solomon is not an allegory about God's love for us or our love for Him. The book is a love story and a celebration of the relationship between a man and a woman in the way intended by God.

Song of Solomon is unapologetically sexual, which would explain why most sermons and Bible studies you hear are not based on these passages. Perhaps an in-depth study of Song of Solomon would not be the most appropriate for children or junior high students; but rather than being uncomfortable with this book of the Bible, we should rejoice that God saw fit for these words to be included. The book of James tells us that every good and perfect gift comes from God. (James 1:17) Yes, people have ruined what God intended by obsessing over sexuality or distorting and corrupting sexuality; but God's intention is nevertheless a good gift that He has given. As with many other aspects of God's creation, man has found a way to adulterate God's blessings.

While God has given us commandments rather than suggestions about how to live, these are given for our good and for our protection. Those who have sinned sexually can experience forgiveness; but they also know the reality of the short and long-term consequences, the very things from which God wanted to protect us in the first place. At the same time, God created us male and female in personality and in anatomy. God created sex and intended for sex to be enjoyed within a marriage relationship. Prudish, legalistic attitudes that view God's blessings as "unclean" do not honor God any more than sexual promiscuity or perversion.

Paul wrote to Timothy, "Now the Spirit expressly says that in later times some will depart from the faith by devoting themselves to deceitful spirits and teachings of demons, through the insincerity of liars whose consciences are seared, who forbid marriage and require abstinence from foods that God created to be received with thanksgiving by those who believe and know the truth. For everything created by God is good, and nothing is to be rejected if it is received with thanksgiving, for it is made holy by the word of God and prayer" (1 Timothy 4:1-5).

What were the ways they were demonstrating they had departed from the faith? They were forbidding marriage and requiring abstinence from certain foods. In other words, they were regarding the good gifts that God had given as evil things to be avoided. What God created is good and not to be rejected! Yes, there are parameters. Yes, there are some conditions. Yes, we have a way of really messing things up. But God gives good gifts for us to enjoy. Sex is not just for procreation but pleasure. Food is not just for nourishment but to be enjoyed. (Especially coffee!) God gave us a life to enjoy, not just an existence.

When we see the pleasures of this life as gifts from God, we come to better understand His heart towards His children. Our obedience to His commands proceeds not out of a religious ritual but from a glad heart that understands His commands are given for our good. Where there are prohibitions, God established them out of love for and protection over us. While we don't live merely for pleasure and every pleasure in this life pales in comparison to what God is preparing for us in heaven, the things we do enjoy in this life point us to a loving, gracious and good God.

HEAD TO HEART

- Do you ever have difficulty seeing pleasures, such as sex and good food, as gifts from God?

- How do you distinguish between a gift from God and gratifying our sinful flesh?

- In what ways can God's good gifts become distractions or hindrances to our relationship with Him?

DAY 23

ISAIAH: WHAT MIGHT HAVE BEEN
READING: ISAIAH 30.

FOCUS: *For thus said the Lord GOD, the Holy One of Israel, "In returning and rest you shall be saved; in quietness and in trust shall be your strength." But you were unwilling, and you said, "No! We will flee upon horses"; therefore you shall flee away; and, "We will ride upon swift steeds"; therefore your pursuers shall be swift. A thousand shall flee at the threat of one; at the threat of five you shall flee, till you are left like a flagstaff on the top of a mountain, like a signal on a hill. Therefore the LORD waits to be gracious to you, and therefore he exalts himself to show mercy to you. For the LORD is a God of justice; blessed are all those who wait for him. For a people shall dwell in Zion, in Jerusalem; you shall weep no more. He will surely be gracious to you at the sound of your cry. As soon as he hears it, he answers you. And though the Lord give you the bread of adversity and the water of affliction, yet your Teacher will not hide himself anymore, but your eyes shall see your Teacher. And your ears shall hear a word behind you, saying, "This is the way, walk in it," when you turn to the right or when you turn to the left.*

Isaiah 30:15-21

For whatever stage of life in which you find yourself — young, old or somewhere in between, none of us wants to look back on our lives with regret. Already there are situations we wish we would have handled differently or choices that we would take back if we could, but hopefully you will never have to look back and think of your life only in terms of what might have been. In ways that are truly beyond our understanding, God created the world in such a way that He is sovereign over all, and yet our choices do matter. His will ultimately will be done; but our decisions, to some degree, still establish the trajectory of our lives.

We read Isaiah 30 from our perspective thousands of years after these words were written. We read of God's mercy and His heart to be gracious to us and guide us as we look to Him. That is our God! But for the people of Judah in Isaiah's day, these were words describing what might have been. God wanted and waited to be gracious to them. He wanted to respond to the sound of their cry. They could have experienced the rest and strength that only come from trusting in Him. But the people of Judah weren't having it – and so they didn't.

The danger they were facing was real. The Assyrians lived up to their reputation. But given the threat, who would Judah rely upon for help? "Ah, stubborn children," declares the LORD, "who carry out a plan, but not mine, and who make an alliance, but not of my Spirit, that they may add sin to sin; who set out to go down to Egypt, without asking for my direction, to take refuge in the protection of Pharaoh and to seek shelter in the shadow of Egypt!" (Isaiah 30:1-2) Instead of trusting the Lord, Judah had trusted in Egypt.

Did they not know or had they forgotten that God had brought their ancestors out of Egypt? Going down to Egypt apparently was appealing because Egypt had horses, but Judah truly was leveraging favor with an enemy who should not have been trusted. If they had turned back to God in their oppression, they could have been saved. Trusting in Him could have been their strength. But then Egypt had *horses*. Yes, that seems ridiculous to us now; but the things in which we place our trust are equally foolish. So God essentially said to them, "Since you want to flee on horses, you will *really* flee on horses." Their strategy, based in human wisdom instead of trust in the Lord, would fail miserably. When God said He waited to be gracious to them, they left Him still waiting.

"And now, go, write it before them on a tablet and inscribe it in a book, that it may be for the time to come as a witness forever. For they are a rebellious people, lying children, children unwilling to hear the instruction of the LORD" (Isaiah 30:8–9). Later generations could come back and read these words and understand the destruction that would happen to Judah and why — and so can we. Truly, the entire Old Testament is a story of what might have been. Their plans failed. Their faith faltered. But God wasn't at all surprised and had a plan of His own.

Today we aren't necessarily tempted to look to Egyptian equines; but many of us still struggle with obsessively strategizing, overthinking and trusting in conventional wisdom when God offers rest through repentance and trusting in Him. Because of Jesus, how much more should we turn away from trusting in human wisdom and strength when God promises blessing if we will wait for Him and look to Him? He probably won't do exactly what we expected, and He probably won't act according to our timing; but He will be gracious at the sound of our cry.

If there is more panic than peace, pray and wait. In the areas in which you want to fret, ask for faith. His voice will guide you, and you will know the right path and when to begin the journey. The temptation will always be there to look to another version of Egypt, but the eventual outcome will be the same. Trust Him. Listen for His voice among all of the noise. In His timing and in His way, you will hear: "This is the way. Walk in it."

HEAD TO HEART

- Have you ever desperately wanted to help someone who clearly did not want your help?

- In what things or people are you tempted to trust rather than rely upon the Lord?

- In what situations do you now wish you had trusted God instead of relying on someone or something else?

DAY 24

JEREMIAH: DON'T FOLLOW YOUR HEART

READING: JEREMIAH 17.

FOCUS: *The heart is deceitful above all things, and desperately sick; who can understand it? "I the LORD search the heart and test the mind to give every man according to his ways, according to the fruit of his deeds."*

Jeremiah 17:9-10

Are you old enough to remember the days of driving while having to use a paper map for directions? Once unfolded, those maps would never fold up the same way again! Aren't you glad there are apps for that now? We think little of mapping technology now, but the convenience is truly amazing – until the GPS app we used fails to get us where we wanted to go. Usually, the directions are flawless and get us where we're going directly; but sometimes we end up somewhere else — completely lost. If this happens once, we might be understanding; but any more than that will mean that next time we use a different GPS. The point is that, if something doesn't get you where you need to go, you need to find a better source for directions.

"Just follow your heart." The expression is heard all too often in our world today and is represented as sage advice. But is your heart always right? When people say, "follow your heart," they typically are referring to feelings; so the counsel being offered is simply to do what your feelings are telling you to do. That mantra has a strong appeal to people today because they are being encouraged not only to determine what is right for themselves but determine what is true. Similarly, the message of movies and other media is to find *your* truth. So, apparently, we just follow our hearts to find our truth. *No wonder.*

Are we surprised this isn't working out so well? People are following their hearts right into destruction. Our feelings and emotions are gifts from God and the way He chose to create us, but how we might feel in a given moment does not determine what is right or true. Truth is not determined by our feelings or opinions — no matter how real they are to us in the moment.

God says the human heart is deceitful and desperately sick. Being that God formed our hearts – both the one that pumps our blood as well as our soul and emotions, He certainly would know. Our hearts are neither the standard of truth nor the source of direction because we simply can't trust them. We tend to rationalize things we should not do and have the ability to deceive even ourselves. Our feelings also change – often over the passing of time but sometimes from moment to moment. That is not to suggest that we simply ignore our feelings or emotions, but they are not ultimate – God is.

He has given us His Word, and His word is truth. We evaluate thoughts, actions, motivations and priorities based on what Scripture says — not based on what we think our heart is saying. This is unpopular in the world today as many would dismiss the idea of making a "faith-based" decision or holding to a "faith-based" value. But everyone is a person of faith. The only difference is where or in what is that faith placed. If someone rejects God and His Word as the source of authority, they are placing their faith in someone or something else.

Some argue they are led only by science and demonstrable facts. The problem is there are plenty of things in this life (and more in the next) that cannot be verified by science. When people try to hide behind so-called science to justify setting themselves up as the ultimate authority, they are following a philosophy rather than science anyway. They are putting a great deal of faith in their own philosophy, the following of their own hearts. People today act as though "just follow your heart" is new and innovative, but everyone doing what was right in their own eyes was disastrous thousands of years ago (see Judges) and remains a recipe for disaster now.

Of course, this can take time. The truth doesn't always emerge right away, and following our own hearts doesn't always entail immediate disaster. We know that sin can be enjoyable for a season. We've observed that something can start out well before eventually ending terribly. You didn't know you were going the wrong way until you didn't get where you wanted to be. In contrast, what God wants us to do often does not make sense or feel good to us. In fact, if everything you are doing makes perfect sense, never makes you uncomfortable and doesn't require you to trust God at a deeper level than before, you may very well be following your heart instead of God's Word.

Ultimately, we will trust God or trust in ourselves. We will trust in the Lord with all of our hearts, or we will lean on our own understanding. (Proverbs 3:5-6) Our hearts can't be trusted, but God never intended for us to follow our own way.

"Blessed is the man who trusts in the LORD, whose trust is the LORD. He is like a tree planted by water, that sends out its roots by the stream, and does not fear when heat comes, for its leaves remain green, and is not anxious in the year of drought, for it does not cease to bear fruit." (Jeremiah 17:7–8)

HEAD TO HEART

- In what ways have you trusted your own understanding or feelings — only to regret doing so later?

- What other clichés and worldly wisdom do you hear being pushed today?

- What should you do when you don't want to follow your heart but don't have a clear direction from God either?

DAY 25

LAMENTATIONS: HOPE IN THE RUBBLE

READING: LAMENTATIONS 3.

FOCUS: *But this I call to mind, and therefore I have hope: The steadfast love of the LORD never ceases; his mercies never come to an end; they are new every morning; great is your faithfulness. "The LORD is my portion," says my soul, "therefore I will hope in him." The LORD is good to those who wait for him, to the soul who seeks him. It is good that one should wait quietly for the salvation of the LORD. It is good for a man that he bear the yoke in his youth. Let him sit alone in silence when it is laid on him; let him put his mouth in the dust—there may yet be hope; let him give his cheek to the one who strikes, and let him be filled with insults. For the Lord will not cast off forever, but, though he cause grief, he will have compassion according to the abundance of his steadfast love; for he does not afflict from his heart or grieve the children of men.*

Lamentations 3:21-33

This book of the Bible wasn't called Lamentations without reason. If you're having such a glorious day that Lamentations seems overly dreary and gloomy, be sure to give thanks and savor the moment. And fear not! The day or the year or the season will unavoidably arrive when these lamentations and other Scriptures — like the Psalms of lament (Psalms 3, 4, 5, 13, etc.) — will connect with you as never before.

Thankfully, not every day is dark. Not every season is overwhelming. We enjoy good days and times of blessing. God truly blesses and graces us far beyond what we deserve. And as much as we might wish that our lives consisted only of the enjoyable seasons, we truly wouldn't enjoy our blessings without the trials and difficulties to provide the contrast and foster thankfulness. Let's not underestimate our ability to feel entitled and deserving when what we are receiving is far better than what we deserve.

For those reasons, when we know the storm is coming, wisdom would entail that we prepare. Do you have a "war chest" of Scriptures, verses and remembrances set aside in preparation for the dark days? We live in a world and in times of uncertainty, so we do well to be ready for things to happen outside of what we can control. What will encourage your heart when difficult days come? Such sections of Scripture might be generally neglected by readers and almost completely ignored by preachers, but the days will come when we will need them.

Lamentations was written in the aftermath of the destruction of Jerusalem — possibly by Jeremiah or at least heavily influenced by him. These words emerged from some of the darkest days soon after the Babylonians had conquered Judah. The city and the Temple lie in ruins. The long process of restoration that one day would begin was far into the future at this point, and the sense of hopelessness was palpable.

"He has walled me about so that I cannot escape; he has made my chains heavy; though I call and cry for help, he shuts out my prayer; he has blocked my ways with blocks of stones; he has made my paths crooked…He has made my teeth grind on gravel, and made me cower in ashes; my soul is bereft of peace; I have forgotten what happiness is; so I say, 'My endurance has perished; so has my hope from the LORD" (Lamentations 3:7-8, 16-18). Whoever wrote Lamentations, he did not have the joy, joy, joy, joy down in his heart — at least in those moments. And at this time in your life, maybe you don't either.

The situation was so dire that the writer only could reflect and lament; he could not shift his focus to a brighter future because he likely couldn't see one. But in his ponderings, he started remembering. Times had been tough before, but God had been faithful. The situation had never been this bleak; but if God had been faithful before, would He not be now? The circumstances were as bad as they could be, but surely God had remained the same. As bad as things were, could there still be hope for them?

"But this I call to mind." Things passively brought to memory at first led to an active reflection, a rehearsal of God's faithfulness in the past. Calling to mind isn't daydreaming or having a passing thought but deliberately choosing to be mindful of something. He brought to his mind what he already knew, and suddenly he had hope — even among the destruction.

Interestingly, almost right in the middle of Lamentations is this classic and rich passage of Scripture that celebrates God's faithfulness — despite all that has happened. How could he (and we) have hope? "The steadfast love of the LORD never ceases; his mercies never come to an end; they are new every morning; great is your faithfulness." There are plenty of other encouraging Scriptures, but this without a doubt is one for your war chest. Imagine all of the followers of Jesus throughout the centuries who have run to a passage like this and all the things that they were going through and found strength and encouragement. Lamentations is a book of sadness; yet even in that sadness, there is amazing hope. The rubble of the city hadn't suddenly come back together, and nothing circumstantially had changed; but there was hope that God was and is still good.

Aren't you glad that the Scriptures aren't happy all the time? Wasn't God wise to give us words like Lamentations, knowing that we would need hope on the darkest of days? He knew we would need to be reminded that His mercies are new *every* morning. May God be glorified in how we trust and rely on His great faithfulness and unceasing love.

HEAD TO HEART

- How have the so-called "depressing" sections of Scripture encouraged you in your walk with God?

- What other Scriptures are your "go-to" verses in times of trouble?

- In what ways can you call to mind God's goodness when there are other voices trying to distract or discourage you?

DAY 26

EZEKIEL: COMING TO LIFE
READING: EZEKIEL 37.

FOCUS: *The hand of the LORD was upon me, and he brought me out in the Spirit of the LORD and set me down in the middle of the valley; it was full of bones. And he led me around among them, and behold, there were very many on the surface of the valley, and behold, they were very dry. And he said to me, "Son of man, can these bones live?" And I answered, "O Lord GOD, you know." Then he said to me, "Prophesy over these bones, and say to them, O dry bones, hear the word of the LORD. Thus says the Lord GOD to these bones: Behold, I will cause breath to enter you, and you shall live. And I will lay sinews upon you, and will cause flesh to come upon you, and cover you with skin, and put breath in you, and you shall live, and you shall know that I am the LORD." So I prophesied as I was commanded. And as I prophesied, there was a sound, and behold, a rattling, and the bones came together, bone to its bone. And I looked, and behold, there were sinews on them, and flesh had come upon them, and skin had covered them. But there was no breath in them. Then he said to me, "Prophesy to the breath; prophesy, son of man, and say to the breath, Thus says the Lord GOD: Come from the four winds, O breath, and breathe on these slain, that they may live." So I prophesied as he commanded me, and the breath came into them, and they lived and stood on their feet, an exceedingly great army. Then he said to me, "Son of man, these bones are the whole house of Israel. Behold, they say, 'Our bones are dried up, and our hope is lost; we are indeed cut off.' Therefore prophesy, and say to them, Thus says the Lord GOD: Behold, I will open your graves and raise you from your graves, O my people. And I will bring you into the land of Israel. And you shall know that I am the LORD, when I open your graves, and raise you from your graves, O my people. And I will put my Spirit within you, and you shall live, and I will place you in your own* *land. Then you shall know that I am the LORD; I have spoken, and I will do it, declares the LORD."*

Ezekiel 37:1-14

We've all heard stories of a person being resuscitated by someone performing CPR, but any life-saving measure is only effective for a limited amount of time. The prophet Ezekiel would not have known about chest compressions or mouth-to-mouth resuscitation; but in the vision that God showed him, knowing CPR wouldn't have saved anyone anyway. The valley to which God took Ezekiel was full of skeletons, and they were literally "bone dry." No flesh, no sinew and not even a lingering odor – just bones scattered all over.

The scene was a graphic picture in the spiritual realm of what was taking place in the natural realm. Many years before, the northern kingdom of Israel had been destroyed by the Assyrians. The people were carried away and enslaved — never to be restored. By the time of Ezekiel's prophecy, Judah recently had been conquered by the Babylonians. The Temple was destroyed, and the people carried into slavery in Babylon. The unthinkable had happened; and their hopes were as a valley of lifeless, dry bones.

Ezekiel must have felt especially helpless and perplexed when God asked him, "Can these bones live?" But imagine how he must have felt when God told Ezekiel to prophesy to the bones. Speak the Word of the Lord to a field of skeletons? Maybe Ezekiel would have been comforted to know that he would not be the only preacher to preach to a dead congregation! Then amazingly, God reassembled and restored the skeletons; and soon there were bodies everywhere instead of dry bones. But the skeletons only became corpses as they still were missing something vitally important – life. Now God could have given them breath at the same time He restored their bodies; but the vision God gave Ezekiel serves to make an important distinction: there is existence, and there is *life*. Even when God created the man from the dust of the ground, he did not become a *living* creature until God breathed into him. (Genesis 2:7)

An exceedingly great army was restored to life, and hope remained for Judah. God would put His Spirit within His people, breathing life into the dry bones. But the vision Ezekiel saw wasn't simply about the future restoration of Judah. God grants biological life to everyone, but only those who know Him have *life* by the power of the Holy Spirit.

In a similar way, man's religions, at their core, are merely self-help programs which suggest that, if we try harder to do better, then we can achieve right standing with God and merit a place in Heaven. Not only is this impossible for us to accomplish since we are deeply flawed, the whole concept of obligating God by our behavior is a lie. God owes us nothing. Apart from the work of the Holy Spirit in us, we are as dead as the dry bones Ezekiel saw in that valley — even though we are biologically alive.

Here's what the Bible says about our spiritual condition apart from Christ: "And you were *dead* in the trespasses and sins in which you once walked, following the course of this world, following the prince of the power of the air, the spirit that is now at work in the sons of disobedience—among whom we all once lived in the passions of our flesh, carrying out the desires of the body and the mind, and were by nature children of wrath, like the rest of mankind" (Ephesians 2:1-3, emphasis mine). We may be breathing air, walking and talking; but apart from the Holy Spirit giving us life in Christ, we are still room temperature dead.

But the Bible goes on to say, "But God, being rich in mercy, because of the great love with which he loved us, even when we were dead in our trespasses, made us alive together with Christ—by grace you have been saved" (Ephesians 2:4–5). We were dead, but Jesus made us alive in Him — not just improved versions of the same person we were. The Gospel is not a self-help program; Jesus came because we could not help ourselves anymore than a pile of bones could come to life without God breathing life into them. This is also why the Gospel (the Biblical and real Gospel) calls us to come and die to ourselves — not improve ourselves. (Luke 9:23-25) Yes, we want to grow, improve and develop; but our best efforts and greatest successes will never make us right with God or give us life. Ezekiel's vision is a vivid picture of what God has done for us through Jesus and by the power of the Holy Spirit.

HEAD TO HEART

- In what ways have you tried to change or improve but lacked the power to be effective?

- What is wrong with so much of the self-help emphasis that is prevalent today?

- Why does religion or good behavior fail to make a person right with God?

DAY 27

DANIEL: THE CONQUERING CAPTIVE

READING: DANIEL 1.

FOCUS: *As for these four youths, God gave them learning and skill in all literature and wisdom, and Daniel had understanding in all visions and dreams. At the end of the time, when the king had commanded that they should be brought in, the chief of the eunuchs brought them in before Nebuchadnezzar. And the king spoke with them, and among all of them none was found like Daniel, Hananiah, Mishael, and Azariah. Therefore they stood before the king. And in every matter of wisdom and understanding about which the king inquired of them, he found them ten times better than all the magicians and enchanters that were in all his kingdom. And Daniel was there until the first year of King Cyrus.*

Daniel 1:17-21

Sometimes a single verse tells the whole story. What seems like a passing mention at the end of a chapter actually is loaded with meaning. After giving us all of the important details about how Daniel and his friends were carried into Babylonian slavery, about how Daniel effectively resisted the "Babylonian makeover" that was being imposed on him, about how God granted him favor with Nebuchadnezzar who was the most powerful man in the world at that time, the writer of Daniel simply adds, "And Daniel was there until the first year of King Cyrus." In other words, Daniel won.

If anyone could write a manual on what to do the next time your nation is invaded by a powerful empire and you're carried off into slavery and trained in the ways the new nation, then Daniel would be the one to write that manual, with perhaps a little help from his friends. Shadrach, Meshach, Abednego and Daniel were all too young to have caused the Exile that brought about their deportation to Babylon. Those who had gone before them continually had rebelled against the Lord and ignored the word of His prophets, but the young Hebrew men were not immune to the consequences and fallout. Just as God had raised up the Assyrians to conquer Israel, He raised up the Babylonians to conquer Judah.

Much like Joseph who was sold into slavery by his brothers many years before, even Daniel's captors recognized that he was a special young man. We might wonder if being selected to live in the palace and learn the ways of the Babylonians was a curse or a blessing, but that was the opportunity God had set before Daniel. No doubt he wished that he was not in the situation at all, but Daniel made the most of the opportunity over and over again.

God used Daniel powerfully to speak truth to Nebuchadnezzar when the king had strange dreams (Daniel 2) and to warn him when he was about to go into "beast mode" (Daniel 4). But after the powerful Nebuchadnezzar was gone, Daniel remained and was consulted by another Babylonian king. As King Belshazzar trembled when a mysterious hand appeared and wrote on the wall, Daniel was able to read the writing on the wall for him – *literally*. (Daniel 5) By the next day, Daniel not only had outlasted Belshazzar but the Babylonian Empire as well. King Darius ruled the next world empire and was tricked into a scheme that entrapped Daniel. Not only did Daniel survive the lions' den, but he also outlasted Darius, too. (Daniel 6) Chalk up another win.

The Bible doesn't give us all of the details, but history indicates that Daniel "was there" from 605 to at least 539 B.C. through Nebuchadnezzar, Belshazzar, Darius and finally Cyrus. That Cyrus was the Persian king whom God prompted to allow God's people to return to Jerusalem and begin to rebuild. In a natural sense, when Daniel was taken captive as a young man and Jerusalem was being destroyed, he had no earthly reason to expect to live to see the day when the Exile would come to an end. Empires rose and fell while Daniel stood firm and remained.

When the circumstances of your life are not what you would have chosen or expected, God isn't finished. You can't be used by God in a place and setting where you aren't, but God will use you where you are. The victory may not be what you anticipated, but sometimes standing firm and staying true are more of a win than we realize. May we be found faithful and prosper in whatever place God has put us. We never know the impact we might have.

HEAD TO HEART

- How does Daniel's example instruct us as we see our culture becoming increasingly hostile towards God's truth?

- How do we discern when we are to stand firm and when the time has come to get out of a situation?

- What does remaining faithful to God entail for you today?

DAY 28

HOSEA: WHAT'S IN A NAME?
READING: HOSEA 1-2.

FOCUS: *And I will betroth you to me forever. I will betroth you to me in righteousness and in justice, in steadfast love and in mercy. I will betroth you to me in faithfulness. And you shall know the LORD. "And in that day I will answer, declares the LORD, I will answer the heavens, and they shall answer the earth, and the earth shall answer the grain, the wine, and the oil, and they shall answer Jezreel, and I will sow her for myself in the land. And I will have mercy on No Mercy, and I will say to Not My People, 'You are my people'; and he shall say, 'You are my God.'"*

Hosea 2:19-23

Ever since the days of the Bible, children have been named after Biblical characters. That explains why even now we know plenty of Davids, Pauls, Sarahs and Marys. Other Biblical names would be a serious challenge to spell or fit on a birth certificate, so we don't come across many Jehoshaphats or Maher-shalal-hash-bazes. (Isaiah 8:3) But if you were seeking a good Biblical name for your child, you probably would want to choose from another book besides Hosea. Hosea's life experience was an analogy of Israel's relationship with God. Sadly, Hosea endured the repeated adultery of his wife Gomer, which mirrored the spiritual adultery that the Lord endured from His own people.

God obviously knew that His people would be unfaithful to Him, but Hosea also was told in advance. "When the LORD first spoke through Hosea, the LORD said to Hosea, 'Go, take to yourself a wife of whoredom and have children of whoredom, for the land commits great whoredom by forsaking the LORD.' So he went and took Gomer, the daughter of Diblaim, and she conceived and bore him a son" (Hosea 1:2-3).

The first child was named Jezreel. What sets Jezreel apart from the other children born to Gomer was that only Jezreel was clearly Hosea's child. The Bible says that Gomer conceived *and* bore Hosea a son. When Gomer later had a daughter named Lo-Ruhama, the text only says that Gomer conceived and bore a daughter. This also was true for the third child, a son named Lo-Ammi. If the absence of an explicit mention of Hosea being the father of the two younger children was not enough, the three different references to "children of whoredom" (Hosea 2:4, 4:6, 5:7) are even more compelling – and truly saddening.

In addition to the sadness of the circumstances surrounding their births, the names of each of the three children only adds to the weight of the story. God specifically told Hosea what to name the children — even the ones who were more than likely not his own. The name Jezreel, which was likely a wordplay on "Israel" since they sound almost alike, means *scattered*. Jezreel symbolized that God was about to scatter Israel. Jezreel was also the name of the place where Jezebel came to a brutal and gory end. (2 Kings 9:30-37) Lo-Ruhama is a strange name for a daughter but even more so when we learn that the name means "no mercy." Through Hosea, God was announcing that the time for showing mercy to Israel had come to an end and that now only Judah would receive His mercy and help. Finally, the third child, a son, was named Lo-Ammi, which meant "not my people." Through the naming of this child, the Lord was saying to Israel, "for you are not my people, and I am not your God" (Hosea 1:9).

Imagine then Hosea's family portrait. There's Hosea, the woman named Gomer, Scattered, No Mercy and Not My People. When God wants to paint a picture, He really paints a picture. But in Gomer's continued unfaithfulness and in Hosea's willingness to receive her back *and* pay the price to do so, we begin to see the love of God for His people. What God was requiring Hosea to do was impossibly hard, but God was doing the same thing Himself but many times over. Israel had been unfaithful — not on an occasion, not in a moment of temptation or weakness, but as a lifestyle. Scripture minces no words in calling the people of Israel whores. We may turn our nose up at that description, but whoredom is the analogy God used to describe the idolatry of His people. And in many ways, this is our story, too.

The Old Testament Law said that, if a man attacked and violated a virgin and was caught, the man was required to pay the price of marriage to her father, take her as his wife and would never be able to divorce her. (Deuteronomy 22:28-29) (That arrangement may sound less than appealing, but keep in mind that a woman had no means of support on her own in those days.) But watch what God did here! He did not violate her, but she was unfaithful to Him. God had no obligation since she was the unfaithful one, but He paid the price as if He had been the violator to redeem the one who had been unfaithful. And God said, "And I will betroth you to me *forever*. I will betroth you to me in righteousness and in justice, in steadfast love and in mercy. I will betroth you to me in *faithfulness*."

Even more, the ones who had been scattered now would be planted. The ones who had not been showed mercy would receive abundant mercy. He said, "You are My people" to those whom He once had called not My people. If this were true for Israel in the Old Testament, how much more so for those who are in Christ! As Peter wrote to Christians who had been scattered by persecution, "Once you were not a people, but now you are God's people; once you had not received mercy, but now you have received mercy" (1 Peter 2:10). We were far off, but now we have been brought near. (Ephesians 2:13) We were, by nature, children of wrath; but God showed us mercy. (Ephesians 2:3)

What Gomer was to Hosea, we have been to God; but because of Jesus — although we once were Gomer — He has given us a new birth and called us His sons and daughters. We are betrothed to Him forever — not because of our righteousness but because of His mercy.

HEAD TO HEART

- Have you ever thought about your sin and idolatry in terms of adultery? Would doing so help us to feel about sin the way that we should?

- If you were Hosea, what would have kept you from simply walking away?

- Do you think the people of Israel heeded the words of Hosea as he explained what God was saying to them?

DAY 29

JOEL: WHEN GOD COMES TO STAY
READING: JOEL 1-2.

> **FOCUS:** *And it shall come to pass afterward, that I will pour out my Spirit on all flesh; your sons and your daughters shall prophesy, your old men shall dream dreams, and your young men shall see visions. Even on the male and female servants in those days I will pour out my Spirit. And I will show wonders in the heavens and on the earth, blood and fire and columns of smoke. The sun shall be turned to darkness, and the moon to blood, before the great and awesome day of the LORD comes. And it shall come to pass that everyone who calls on the name of the LORD shall be saved. For in Mount Zion and in Jerusalem there shall be those who escape, as the LORD has said, and among the survivors shall be those whom the LORD calls.*
>
> *Joel 2:28-32*

Before we run ahead to what this passage means for us or even to what the words meant to Peter and Paul when they quoted them centuries later, we should consider *first* the original context. Considering what a passage of Scripture meant in its original context first will help us understand what the Scripture means for us today. If that first step is not taken, all kinds of kooky and ridiculous ideas that the Holy Spirit never intended can emerge. As someone once said, a passage of Scripture "doesn't *mean* what it never *meant.*"

With that in view, the exact date and setting for Joel's prophecy isn't certain; but with the details we do have, Joel prophesied at a pivotal time. The first chapter of Joel describes the devastation that resulted from a plague of locusts. Not only were there too many locusts but at least four different kinds. The cutting locust, the swarming locust, the hopping locust and the destroying locust destroyed everything and probably made a whole lot of noise in the process. (Joel 1:4, 10) The plague and the resulting devastation served as an unavoidable call to repentance.

But God wasn't finished with His people nor was He walking away from them. "'Yet even now,' declares the LORD, 'return to me with all your heart, with fasting, with weeping, and with mourning; and rend your hearts and not your garments. Return to the LORD your God, for he is gracious and merciful, slow to anger, and abounding in steadfast love; and he relents over disaster'" (Joel 2:12–13).

The people of God, in turn, did what we don't often see them do – they confessed their sins and turned away from them. And after all the devastation, their repentance changed their situation. "Then the LORD became jealous for his land and had pity on his people. The LORD answered and said to his people, 'Behold, I am sending to you grain, wine, and oil, and you will be satisfied; and I will no more make you a reproach among the nations'" (Joel 2:18-19).

But in the promise to restore the land, God wasn't finished. Where the first part of His promise spoke of physical and material blessings, another part of the promise focused on the spiritual. This promise would be fulfilled much later but would be for much more than just the people of Israel or Judah. God was promising that the day would come when He not only would be with His people but that He would dwell *within* His people.

We can't be certain as to what all of these promises would have meant to Joel's original hearers, but the New Testament gives us tremendous help in seeing what the Holy Spirit intended – *Himself*. Centuries later, God would send His Son; but when His Son had completed the work He came to do, He also would send the Holy Spirit.

After Jesus ascended back to Heaven, when the Holy Spirit came at Pentecost, Peter quoted these exact words from Joel. Peter and the others connected the dots to what Joel had prophesied so many years before, which was now being fulfilled. No doubt, the Christians in the first-century church were amazed to see the prophecies coming to fulfillment and to know that they were a part of what God had promised long before. Unlike the pre-Pentecost days when the Holy Spirit would visit, so to speak, He now would come to live in every believer — just as Jesus had told His disciples. (John 16:5-11)

In the days of the Old Testament, the Spirit of the Lord would come and empower a person in a special way (Judges 14:6; 1 Samuel 10:10); but His presence was not permanently within them in the way that He would indwell those who know Jesus. The Spirit of God was clearly with them on specific occasions, but He clearly had departed at other times. (Judges 16:20; 1 Samuel 16:14)

When Jesus told His disciples that He would be going away soon, they were, of course, saddened; but He assured them it was to their advantage that He was going away because the Holy Spirit then would come soon afterwards. When the Spirit came at Pentecost, He came to stay.

More specifically, God would live within those who know Jesus by the Holy Spirit. When we sense the presence of the Lord, that's the Holy Spirit. When we are convicted about our sin, that's the Holy Spirit. When we are empowered to do what we cannot do in our own strength, that's the Holy Spirit. The Spirit also assures us that we belong to God. (Romans 8:15-16) The same Spirit, Whom Joel prophesied, now lives in us, intercedes for us and glorifies God through us as we daily surrender ourselves to Him.

HEAD TO HEART

- Why do you think God would choose the time that He did to promise the coming of His Spirit?

- What are the implications for us, as believers in Jesus, that the Spirit is not just with us but lives within us?

- Why do we tend to neglect or at least not focus on the Holy Spirit and only talk about the Father and the Son?

DAY 30

AMOS: DON'T SHOOT THE MESSENGER

READING: AMOS 7.

FOCUS: *Then Amaziah the priest of Bethel sent to Jeroboam king of Israel, saying, "Amos has conspired against you in the midst of the house of Israel. The land is not able to bear all his words. For thus Amos has said, "'Jeroboam shall die by the sword, and Israel must go into exile away from his land.'" And Amaziah said to Amos, "O seer, go, flee away to the land of Judah, and eat bread there, and prophesy there, but never again prophesy at Bethel, for it is the king's sanctuary, and it is a temple of the kingdom." Then Amos answered and said to Amaziah, "I was no prophet, nor a prophet's son, but I was a herdsman and a dresser of sycamore figs. But the LORD took me from following the flock, and the LORD said to me, 'Go, prophesy to my people Israel.' Now therefore hear the word of the LORD. "You say, 'Do not prophesy against Israel, and do not preach against the house of Isaac.' Therefore thus says the LORD: "'Your wife shall be a prostitute in the city, and your sons and your daughters shall fall by the sword, and your land shall be divided up with a measuring line; you yourself shall die in an unclean land, and Israel shall surely go into exile away from its land.'"*

Amos 7:10-17

Amos had a rough time, but maybe he would be happy to know that truth tellers aren't all that popular today either. Even among religious people, the truth isn't always welcomed — even when that truth comes from God. Because Amos told the truth of impending judgment, he succeeded in upsetting Amaziah, the high priest. Had Amos known that Jesus would later anger almost all of the religious leaders, he might have rejoiced that he was in good company.

God had given Amos a series of visions — each a warning that judgment was coming on the people of Israel. When God showed Amos a plumb line (the ancestor of laser levels), He was revealing that Israel was crooked and drastically out of alignment with what God had required of His people. King Jeroboam (the second king of Israel by this name) was being held directly responsible for the decline in Israel; and the Lord said, "and I will rise against the house of Jeroboam with the sword" (Amos 7:9).

Of all people, wouldn't the high priest *want* everyone to hear the Word of the Lord? Sadly, not in this case. Amaziah was not at all appreciative of Amos or the message he brought and told Amos to go prophesy in Judah if Amos thought he had something to say. (King Jeroboam II was likely not thrilled either.) But when Amaziah mentioned that Amos should go and "eat bread" in Judah, he was suggesting that Amos merely was prophesying for money and personal gain. More than likely, you have seen something like this before as this same tactic is often used today. Rather than acknowledge any personal wrongdoing, just accuse the other person of the same wrong that you're doing. Clearly, if anyone was seeking personal gain, Amaziah was the guilty one who apparently had learned a form of "gaslighting" before the term ever had been invented.

Amos famously replied, "I'm not a prophet nor the son of a prophet, but God called me away from my flocks to go and prophesy." Amos hadn't signed up for any of this. He likely was making a respectable living and perhaps enjoying his life when God called him. And unlike others whom God had called, Amos apparently obeyed immediately. Now God had Amos sharing an unwelcome message to an unreceptive audience. No, Amos wasn't doing this for the money or the fame. Amos wasn't quite finished either.

Since Amaziah the high priest initially was so opposed to the Word of the Lord through Amos, God gave Amos another word for Amaziah that likely wasn't received well either: "Your wife will be a prostitute, your children will be killed, your land will be divided, and you and many others will die as slaves in a foreign land." Denying or suppressing the truth doesn't change the truth or make it all go away (see Romans 1). Refusing to hear and accept the truth leads to a worsening of consequences since ignorance no longer can be an excuse.

Amos lived and died a long time ago, but resistance to the truth is alive and well. Atheists know there is a God – they simply don't *want* there to be a God and live as though He doesn't exist. But closer to home, people will flock to churches who simply repeat how much God loves us and wants to bless us. God does love us and does want to bless us, but often His love and blessing come in the form of suffering and difficulty. God also loves us enough as His children to bring discipline and correction and to call us to repentance. None of the believers we read about in the New Testament walked an easy, prosperous road. They suffered and endured, and God loved each of them.

From Amos and others like him, we learn to speak the truth even when that truth is unpopular and to heed those who speak the truth to us. Even for those who go to church at every opportunity — if we are never convicted about an area of our lives or challenged to consider trials as purposeful gifts, something is sorely missing — God's truth. The Gospel isn't truly good news unless and until we've accepted the bad news first.

HEAD TO HEART

- What motivates people to deny and suppress the truth, especially when God is speaking?

- On what occasions were you told something you knew to be true, but you didn't want to hear it?

- Who do you see as a "prophet" in your life who can say the things that you need to hear the most?

DAY 31

OBADIAH: WHO CARES?

READING: THE ENTIRE BOOK OF OBADIAH!

FOCUS: *The vision of Obadiah. Thus says the Lord GOD concerning Edom: We have heard a report from the LORD, and a messenger has been sent among the nations: "Rise up! Let us rise against her for battle!" Behold, I will make you small among the nations; you shall be utterly despised. The pride of your heart has deceived you, you who live in the clefts of the rock, in your lofty dwelling, who say in your heart, "Who will bring me down to the ground?" Though you soar aloft like the eagle, though your nest is set among the stars, from there I will bring you down, declares the LORD.*

Obadiah 1-4

Obadiah is one of the Minor Prophets, the last 12 books of the Old Testament with the strange names. The messages of the Minor Prophets are powerful and important but relatively brief. (Do you know any preachers who could learn something from that?) But even among the Minor Prophets, Obadiah probably wins the contest for being the least known among the least known. As we will see, none of the Minor Prophets could win the Miss Congeniality Award; but Obadiah likely would win the Most Obscure.

For starters, Obadiah's prophecy is the shortest book (no chapters – just verses!) in the Old Testament. The specific Obadiah who wrote the book of Obadiah is difficult to pinpoint because the Scripture mentions many different people named Obadiah. Finally, Obadiah's message from God was not even directed at God's people. He was a Hebrew prophet who did not prophesy to the Hebrews.

Instead Obadiah spoke the Word of the Lord to Edom, a nation to the southeast of Jerusalem whose people were descendants of Esau and distant relatives of the people of Judah. (Genesis 36) To the Edomites,

God said, "I will bring you down." Before we consider why God was bringing judgment on the Edomites, we probably would benefit from asking another question first: *Who cares?*

Now we know that we're supposed to care at some level because the book of Obadiah is in the Bible; but besides that, why does any of this matter? Without being purposely disrespectful or irreverent, the Edomites simply aren't important to us. But that's part of the charm and beauty of this short and generally unknown book. We read things about which we don't know and honestly don't care but, in the process, discover that God did care.

Maybe we aren't too concerned that God brought judgment on the Edomites, but we do well to pay attention to *why* He did. As best we can tell, Obadiah likely was speaking for the Lord soon after the Babylonians had conquered Judah and destroyed Jerusalem. These were the darkest of days for God's people. Having ignored all of the warnings, they now had received the consequences of idolatry and turning away from the Lord. Just like Israel before them, the people of Judah had "sown the wind and reaped the whirlwind" (Hosea 8:7). They were defeated and exiled, and they knew why.

But as the axe fell on Jerusalem, the Edomites celebrated and plundered. Arrogantly assuming something like that never could happen to them, the Edomites gloated and captured for themselves some of the stragglers fleeing the city. They kicked God's people when they already were down. But God cared.

Even in the aftermath of God's judgment of sending His people into exile, God wanted the Edomites to understand: "For the day of the LORD is near upon all the nations. As you have done, it shall be done to you; your deeds shall return on your own head" (Obadiah 15). For Judah, there one day would be a time of restoration; but Edom would be destroyed and never rise again.

Still, we don't really care about the Edomites. Even if they got what was coming to them, great; but that doesn't matter right now. But that's the whole point — God cared; and because He cared, God acted.

The reason we care (even if we thought we didn't) is because reading about God speaking judgment on the Edomites through this almost anonymous prophet offers us the reassurance that God is for His people, that evil will not prevail and that evildoers will get what is coming to them. There is a God in Heaven Who is working everything according to the counsel of His will so that we can be comforted to know that, just as God handled the Edomite situation so long ago, He also will work in our situation, too.

HEAD TO HEART

- Do you sometimes wonder why God put such obscure and even strange things in His Word?

- Are you sometimes tempted to rejoice when someone seems to be getting retribution? How should we handle these situations?

- Do you live in the assurance that God cares for you, or do you typically look to take matters into your own hands?

DAY 32

JONAH: WHEN GOD LOVES YOUR ENEMIES

READING: JONAH 3-4.

FOCUS: *When God saw what they did, how they turned from their evil way, God relented of the disaster that he had said he would do to them, and he did not do it. But it displeased Jonah exceedingly, and he was angry. And he prayed to the LORD and said, "O LORD, is not this what I said when I was yet in my country? That is why I made haste to flee to Tarshish; for I knew that you are a gracious God and merciful, slow to anger and abounding in steadfast love, and relenting from disaster. Therefore now, O LORD, please take my life from me, for it is better for me to die than to live." And the LORD said, "Do you do well to be angry?"*

Jonah 3:10-4:4

In our modern, sophisticated culture that claims nothing can be true that is not supported by science, the story of Jonah often is viewed as a myth or a fairy tale. After all, are we really to believe that a large fish actually swallowed a man alive and that the man survived for several days inside the fish until he was vomited out? Well, Jesus did. "For just as Jonah was three days and three nights in the belly of the great fish, so will the Son of Man be three days and three nights in the heart of the earth" (Matthew 12:40). Jesus referred to Jonah as an historical figure and his being swallowed up as an historical event. If we don't believe Him on that point, can He be believed on anything else? We don't get to pick and choose according to our preferences.

When God spoke to Jonah and said, "Arise, go to Nineveh, that great city, and call out against it, for their evil has come up before me" (Jonah 1:2), we might assume that Jonah's disobedient response was based in fear. Nineveh was the main city of the Assyrians; and all political correctness aside, the Assyrians were not nice people. They would come to be known especially for the cruelty they inflicted on the nations they conquered as they established their empire. Jonah had good reason to be fearful of the Ninevites, but that wasn't the reason he bought a ticket for a ship going in the opposite direction.

When God told Jonah to go to the Ninevites, this was not the first time He had spoken to or through Jonah, so the command was not totally unexpected or unprecedented. Previously, Jonah had spoken the Word of the Lord to Jeroboam (II), the evil king of Israel; and Jeroboam perhaps had surprisingly acted upon what Jonah had revealed from the Lord. (2 Kings 14:23-25) Surely, Jonah knew that he was taking a risk by speaking the Word of the Lord to an evil king; but on that occasion, Jonah obeyed. He could not have been surprised when God wanted to use him to speak His Word again.

No, Jonah wasn't afraid to speak for God because he already had done so. The issue was that Jonah just didn't like his new assignment. And here is the place at which many of us can relate to Jonah since you, too, may be less than delighted with your current assignment. But hopefully, none of us will follow Jonah's lead.

Evidently, Jonah was lacking in wise counsel during this season of his life because no wise person would have advised Jonah to try to flee from God by sailing in the opposite direction. Going the opposite way when you see someone in the store and don't want to talk to them is often effective, but the strategy never works with God. You might as well close your eyes tightly in hopes that God won't be able to see you.

But what really drove Jonah's disobedience — if not fear or a lack of boldness? Why was Jonah so desperate to avoid the assignment? After Jonah fled from the Lord, we find out why. After Jonah witnessed firsthand the digestive processes of a large fish, we find out his real motivation. After Jonah finally preached to the Ninevites and they surprisingly heeded his words and repented, we learn from Jonah's words to the Lord what was really going on here. Ready?

Jonah didn't *like* the Ninevites.

All that happened in Jonah's story was the result of his despising the people of Nineveh. The problem for Jonah is that God didn't share those feelings. Truly, Jonah didn't even *want* the Ninevites to repent. What frightened Jonah even more than the Ninevites was the possibility that the Ninevites might receive his message, turn from wickedness and receive God's mercy. Jonah must have been terribly disappointed when the Ninevites did exactly that. "That is why I made haste to flee to Tarshish; for I knew that you are a gracious God and merciful, slow to anger and abounding in steadfast love, and relenting from disaster."

"God, I *knew* this was going to happen. It's just like You to show mercy to people like that!" We don't know who wrote the book of Jonah, but the details certainly paint Jonah in an unflattering light. But if Jonah didn't compose the book himself, he must have revealed the ugly details about himself to the person who did. Maybe Jonah learned his lesson. Maybe that's the reason the Holy Spirit moved Jonah (or someone) to tell the story. What a merciful God to show compassion to the Ninevites... and to Jonah... and to us.

Will it be okay with you if God wants to show mercy instead of judgment to certain others — even those you don't like? Jonah's story can be an indictment of our attitudes toward other people. Yes, their sin or weakness or failure is a huge problem but nothing that God's mercy cannot overcome. Like Jonah, often we'd rather see them get what's coming to them rather than receiving His mercy in the way that we have. Of course, we don't expect that God simply will overlook sin; but do we pray and hope that they will repent and receive mercy instead of judgment while there is still time? Do you mind if God shows *them* His mercy, too? Shouldn't God be glorified by *those people*, too?

HEAD TO HEART

- Who are the "Ninevites" for you?

- In what ways have you had an attitude like Jonah's? Can you pray for God's justice and have compassion at the same time?

- Does the mercy that God has shown to you truly move you to be merciful to others?

DAY 33

MICAH: LIGHT IN THE DARKNESS
READING: MICAH 7.

FOCUS: *But as for me, I will look to the LORD; I will wait for the God of my salvation; my God will hear me. Rejoice not over me, O my enemy; when I fall, I shall rise; when I sit in darkness, the LORD will be a light to me. I will bear the indignation of the LORD because I have sinned against him, until he pleads my cause and executes judgment for me. He will bring me out to the light; I shall look upon his vindication. Then my enemy will see, and shame will cover her who said to me, "Where is the LORD your God?" My eyes will look upon her; now she will be trampled down like the mire of the streets.*

Micah 7:7-10

As Job and others could attest, sometimes the worst thing does happen. We are not certain whether Micah was describing a situation that already had occurred or if he was referring to a day of judgment that would come on another day. (Micah 4:10) Either way, the worst-case scenario had become the present reality. But even in the darkness, Micah expressed a quiet but confident assurance in the goodness of God. We can hope that his trust in the Lord inspired the same faith among the people of Judah and the same for us centuries later. The Word of God has the astounding ability to do that.

After the judgment had fallen and the things concerning which Micah had been warning the people had come, with a renewed focus, Micah again looked to the Lord. "I will look. . .I will wait. . .God will hear." That simple formula is profound and instructive on our worst days as well. Even though the circumstances could not have looked any worse, Micah possessed the boldness and humility to believe that not only could God save — He *would* save.

When Micah begins, "Rejoice not over me, O my enemy," he likely is voicing the sentiment of the people or at least a remnant of them. Even if we are not certain as to all of the specifics, they clearly had seen God's judgment fall and were living in the aftermath. They indeed had fallen but had come to the place of acknowledging and accepting that they had sinned and that God's actions were justified. And yet they now had hope that seemed to be absent before the calamity.

"When I fall, I shall rise."

"When I sit in darkness, the LORD will be a light to me."

Is that how we sound on our worst days? But more than just having a rough time, they knew that their pain mostly was self-inflicted. God had warned. They had ignored. They had sinned. After enough cycles of that monotonous routine, God had enough. Micah and the others understood they were bearing the indignation of the Lord as a direct result of their actions and attitudes. But they understood something else, and that understanding provided a glorious hope.

Although they had sinned against God, they held to the belief that God Himself would be the One to plead their cause. When the Judge is also the One Who pleads your cause, there is hope — even when you are guilty as sin. As Micah would later proclaim: "Who is a God like you, pardoning iniquity and passing over transgression for the remnant of his inheritance? He does not retain his anger forever, because he delights in steadfast love. He will again have compassion on us; he will tread our iniquities underfoot. You will cast all our sins into the depths of the sea. You will show faithfulness to Jacob and steadfast love to Abraham, as you have sworn to our fathers from the days of old" (Micah 7:18-20).

But there is still more. Haven't you also heard the voice of the enemy in the times when you sat in darkness? Remember that accusing voice that says, "Where is God *now*? If God is so good, why are you in such a bad place? You trusted God, but how did that work out for you?" The hope and assurance were that not only would God plead their cause, but He also would bring vindication as their enemies would be trampled like mud in the street. Truly, God was the Light in their darkness.

But how much more is this true for us in Christ! He already has taken our place. God already has executed His judgment – not on us but on His Son. Romans 8:1 assures us, "There is therefore now no condemnation for those who are in Christ Jesus." Colossians 2:13-15 tells us what God has done about that accusing voice: "And you, who were dead in your trespasses and the uncircumcision of your flesh, God made alive together with him, having forgiven us all our trespasses, by canceling the record of debt that stood against us with its legal demands. This he set aside, nailing it to the cross. He disarmed the rulers and authorities and put them to open shame, by triumphing over them in him."

Once and for all, God has trampled our enemy like mud in the street. Jesus walked through the darkness for us; but He walked out of the darkness, too! Because He did, the darkness of our worst days, our deepest scars and even our self-inflicted wounds will not overcome the Light.

HEAD TO HEART

- What occasion or season of your life most closely parallels what Micah describes?

- When you sin, do you tend to run to God or try to avoid Him?

- How do you effectively respond to the voice of the enemy that accuses God and questions your faith in Him?

DAY 34

NAHUM: GOD IS WHO HE IS
READING: NAHUM 1.

FOCUS: *The LORD is a jealous and avenging God; the LORD is avenging and wrathful; the LORD takes vengeance on his adversaries and keeps wrath for his enemies. The LORD is slow to anger and great in power, and the LORD will by no means clear the guilty. His way is in whirlwind and storm, and the clouds are the dust of his feet...Who can stand before his indignation? Who can endure the heat of his anger? His wrath is poured out like fire, and the rocks are broken into pieces by him. The LORD is good, a stronghold in the day of trouble; he knows those who take refuge in him. But with an overflowing flood he will make a complete end of the adversaries, and will pursue his enemies into darkness.*

Nahum 1:2-3, 6-8

If Obadiah is the most obscure Old Testament book, Nahum probably finishes a close second. Part of the reason the Minor Prophets are read or preached rarely is because they can be difficult to understand and, therefore, are avoided. At the same time, we somehow find a way to use technology and devices that we don't fully understand either. We must see the importance and the relevance to make the effort, or we will end up reading Nahum and the other prophets like we're reading names in a phone book — if we read them at all.

Yes, the Minor Prophets are challenging; but another unspoken reason may be the more dominant cause of avoiding Nahum and the others. Most would not want to admit to this idea, but people may not necessarily *like* the God they encounter there. Nahum's description of God includes attributes like jealousy, avenging and wrathful. Do you have room in your understanding of God for those characteristics? We don't get to worship the God of our choosing or create God in our image or in the image of what we'd like for Him to be. God is Who He is.

Nahum apparently had never been to preaching class and learned that a message is supposed to start with a captivating illustration or a comical anecdote to grab the attention of the listeners. Imagine hearing a sermon that begins, "The LORD is a jealous and avenging God; the LORD is avenging and wrathful. . . ." Evidently, the urgency and gravity of the message propelled Nahum to skip the hors d'oeuvres and get right to the main course. But why this description? Why was God unleashing His wrath?

About a century before Nahum, the more famous prophet Jonah reluctantly had warned the people of the Assyrian capital city of Nineveh about God's impending judgment. Much to our surprise and much to Jonah's disappointment, the Ninevites heeded the message and turned from their evil ways. God granted the people of Nineveh mercy and a measure of repentance in Jonah's day, but the fruits of that repentance didn't last for long.

After the days of Jonah, the Assyrians later destroyed the northern kingdom of Israel. They were especially known for their brutality and cruelty in conquering their enemies. Even though God had used them to bring judgment on Israel, He also would bring His judgment to bear on the Assyrians. Nothing had escaped His notice nor would anyone guilty escape His wrath. The cruelty inflicted by the Assyrians, in turn, was inflicted back on them when they were conquered by the Babylonians.

But while these historical events were the backdrop of Nahum's prophecy and they help us understand his message, Nahum, more importantly, wrote about the attributes of God. Thousands of years have passed, and times are different; but God has remained the same. What remains true about God is that He is jealous and avenging and wrathful. He stores up wrath for His enemies. Although He is slow to anger, He will not leave the guilty unpunished forever. His way is in the whirlwind and the storm, which conveys devastation and destruction

— not the gentleness of a light summer breeze.

Some will object to this harsher description of God and would prefer a more tame, docile God; but God's love and God's wrath go hand in hand. You probably don't need anyone to remind you that evil exists in this world — not just people making bad choices, mistakes or misdemeanors — but pure evil. Where God has dealt with evil on a smaller scale in the past, the day is coming in which He will destroy evil with ferocity and finality.

When we understand that God is all powerful, flawlessly holy and perfect in righteousness, we begin to grasp how astonishing is the truth that He is our refuge. We should be the recipients of His wrath; but because of His grace, He protects us not only from His wrath but from every evil as well. Even more, the righteous fury of an avenging and wrathful God was not merely a threat or warning but truly and fully was poured out on Jesus. He took the wrath we deserved so that we could know Him and take refuge in Him. Because that wrath was poured out on Jesus, no wrath or condemnation remains for those who trust in Him.

The Lord is good, but He also is to be reverenced and feared. He is a God of love, but He is also a God of vengeance. We praise Him because He is slow to anger but also great in power. Nahum reminds us that we serve the Almighty God.

HEAD TO HEART

- What does it mean for God to be jealous over His people? Isn't jealousy a negative thing?
- How do we balance an intimate love for God with an appropriate fear of God?
- What should you do when you encounter a truth or an attribute of God that makes you uncomfortable?

DAY 35

HABAKKUK: WATCHING AND WAITING

READING: HABAKKUK 2.

FOCUS: *I will take my stand at my watchpost and station myself on the tower, and look out to see what he will say to me, and what I will answer concerning my complaint. And the LORD answered me: "Write the vision; make it plain on tablets, so he may run who reads it. For still the vision awaits its appointed time; it hastens to the end—it will not lie. If it seems slow, wait for it; it will surely come; it will not delay. Behold, his soul is puffed up; it is not upright within him, but the righteous shall live by his faith."*

Habakkuk 2:1-4

"Is it okay to complain to God?" Almost all of us either raise or encounter that question somewhere along the way in our journey with the Lord. Like the answer to many other questions, the answer depends on certain conditions. Is our posture towards God more *asking* because we truly don't understand, or are we *accusing* God because we think that we deserve better treatment? We can be encouraged and comforted to know that the Holy Spirit inspired the writers of Scripture to include their complaints to God and their struggles to understand what He was doing (or not doing). Apparently, He knew that we might have some complaints of our own.

When our limited perception suggests that God is acting out of character or isn't doing what we think He should be doing, we need to consider two things. Does God have information and understanding that we don't? Is there more to God than what we understand? In any event, we can't take our standards of right and wrong and try to apply them to God. We are the ones with limited understanding. Not only is what God doing always right, but whatever He does is also *good*.

When Habakkuk brought his complaints to God, he undoubtedly knew that he was being bold, but he nevertheless was expecting a response. At the same time, Habakkuk knew he could not force or manipulate God to answer. Holding his breath or pounding his fists on the floor might make Habakkuk blue and tired, but those negotiation tactics would not rush God along. Habakkuk asked and now he would wait. But in the asking, Habakkuk did go to God instead of relying on his own understanding. That's a step we often skip. We talk to God about the situation, and then we wait. We don't know how long Habakkuk waited for a response, but God's answer came only when God was ready.

Whether the answer came quickly or slowly, God answered Habakkuk, and His response was gentle, considering Habakkuk's boldness. God was gracious in understanding that Habakkuk didn't understand. Isn't that good to know as you bring your questions and complaints to God? Now God doesn't often tell someone to write something down on tablets; so when He does, we should pay attention. He was telling Habakkuk, "Don't just hear this word — write it down and then run with it. In other words, proclaim this word and make it known."

God was assuring Habakkuk this wasn't the end of the story. Even though all appearances indicated nothing was happening, God was at work and doing more than Habakkuk could understand. The suspense has been building — God told Habakkuk to get ready and write this down. This is going to be important, so what is the message?

"Behold, his soul is puffed up; it is not upright within him, but the righteous shall live by his faith."

We have to wonder if Habakkuk didn't think to himself, "Is that *it*?" But when we ponder the response, the word to Habakkuk was powerful. Not only did the word impact Habakkuk, but the phrase "the righteous shall live by (his) faith" changed the world. Centuries later, Paul and the writer of Hebrews quoted these words as they expounded the implications of the Gospel. (Romans 1:17; Galatians 3:11; Hebrews 10:38)

"The righteous will live by faith" was also one of the major themes and rallying cries of the Protestant Reformation 1,500 years later.

What was God saying to Habakkuk and to us? The way to have a relationship with Him is through faith. In contrast, the arrogant will lean on their own understanding and do what is right in their own eyes. Faith will characterize the righteous – not behavior, not acts of service, but trust in the Lord. A Godly lifestyle results from and demonstrates our faith.

This faith is simply believing in God's character and in His promises. We trust that God is good when our circumstances seem to say the opposite. Remember the serpent's tactic in the Garden of Eden was to get Adam and Eve to doubt God's goodness. They sinned because they bought into the lie that God was withholding something good from them. (Genesis 3:1-7) Ultimately, every time we sin, our sin stems from a failure to believe what God has promised.

But in Habakkuk's story, we see a great picture of living by faith. We trust God not only to do what is right and loving but also trust His timing for when He will act. Habakkuk stationed himself on the watchpost, watching and waiting in faith for God to speak and for God to act. Chances are you have stood on that same watchpost, and you may be there even today. This is the opportunity to see your life with eyes of faith and to trust Him.

Someday we won't need faith anymore; all will be sight. As we watch and wait, may God someday say to us, "You may have messed up plenty of times, but You trusted Me. What I was doing made no sense to you, but you believed Me. What I allowed in your life sometimes seemed senseless and even cruel, but you rested in My goodness and trusted in My promises."

We don't simply believe that everything is all going to work out; but rather, going all in, we trust that God is Who He says He is and that every one of His promises are true. This is watching and waiting in faith.

HEAD TO HEART

- How do you know if you are asking questions to God or accusing God of wrongdoing?

- What do you do when you are asking God for answers and those answers are not yet being revealed?

- In what specific ways are you watching and waiting for God right now?

DAY 36

ZEPHANIAH: THE PURGING OF PRIDE
READING: ZEPHANIAH 3.

FOCUS: *On that day you shall not be put to shame because of the deeds by which you have rebelled against me; for then I will remove from your midst your proudly exultant ones, and you shall no longer be haughty in my holy mountain. But I will leave in your midst a people humble and lowly. They shall seek refuge in the name of the LORD, those who are left in Israel; they shall do no injustice and speak no lies, nor shall there be found in their mouth a deceitful tongue. For they shall graze and lie down, and none shall make them afraid. Sing aloud, O daughter of Zion; shout, O Israel! Rejoice and exult with all your heart, O daughter of Jerusalem! The LORD has taken away the judgments against you; he has cleared away your enemies. The King of Israel, the LORD, is in your midst; you shall never again fear evil. On that day it shall be said to Jerusalem: "Fear not, O Zion; let not your hands grow weak. The LORD your God is in your midst, a mighty one who will save; he will rejoice over you with gladness; he will quiet you by his love; he will exult over you with loud singing."*

Zephaniah 3:11-17

The third chapter of Zephaniah is quite a relief after the first two chapters of wrath and judgment. Like many of the other Old Testament prophets, Zephaniah must have believed in giving the bad news before the good news. The word of the Lord began with, "I will utterly sweep away everything from the face of the earth" (Zephaniah 1:2) and generally remained on that same theme for two chapters. If Zephaniah was attempting to start out on an ominous tone, he succeeded. The Day of the Lord was at hand, and the wrath of God was coming – not exactly tidings of comfort and joy, comfort and joy.

While Judah was the first in line for judgment, God was making clear that Judah's enemies would not escape His wrath either. The judgment would be on an equal-opportunity basis. The Babylonians soon would begin invading Jerusalem, and the period of the Exile would begin; but was there escape for *anyone*? The mercy of God would ensure there was still a remnant among His people. Doom was on the horizon, and yet hope remained.

The first glimmer of this hope came in Zephaniah 2:3 — even as the surrounding nations were about to receive their due. "Seek the LORD, all you humble of the land, who do his just commands; seek righteousness; seek humility; perhaps you may be hidden on the day of the anger of the LORD." The Lord was waiting for His people to humble themselves and repent. While the majority would fail to heed the warning, no one could claim that the opportunity wasn't presented.

So who would be spared? Only the ones who would humble themselves and recognize how desperately they needed the Lord. Rather than haughtiness and self-reliance, God would be their refuge. The heart of God was to spare His people and rescue them from impending judgment, but mercy would not be shown to those who were "proudly exultant" and saw no need for His rule in their lives. But this humility was not merely a matter of words but was demonstrated in how they lived. Their meekness would be displayed in maintaining justice and integrity. We've all known fake people who try to impress us with how deeply humble they are, but authentic humility unavoidably results in acting justly and treating others graciously.

Centuries later, an apostle who himself had learned some hard lessons about humility wrote, "Humble yourselves, therefore, under the mighty hand of God so that at the proper time he may exalt you, casting all your anxieties on him, because he cares for you." (1 Peter 5:6-7). Humility paves the way for God to work in our lives and for us to experience all that He is for us in Jesus. We rest in the peace that only He can give. We have no need to be afraid because of His assurance that He will be with us. And perhaps best of all, all our sins and failures are taken away. We are no longer objects of His wrath. (Ephesians 2:1-3) What Zephaniah knew only partially, we get to see much more completely in the light of Jesus.

Even against the backdrop of wrath and judgment, the book of Zephaniah provides us with one of the most powerful descriptions of God's love for His children in all of the Bible. "The LORD your God is in your midst, a mighty one who will save; he will rejoice over you with gladness; he will quiet you by his love; he will exult over you with loud singing." The very thought of God celebrating us, rejoicing over us, singing over us does not point to our worth but to His! We should be humbled in the light of His mercy and love for us. Knowing that we are completely undeserving and unworthy only magnifies the goodness of God towards His people. Our whole lives, our very existence, then, are for the praise of His glory.

HEAD TO HEART

- What are the main ways that you struggle with pride? Do you think you are aware of all these areas?

- Given that there are plenty of sinful attitudes, why is God so opposed to pride?

- Do you ever have trouble believing that God truly rejoices over *you*? Why do we sometimes struggle to truly embrace this truth?

DAY 37

HAGGAI: WHEN GOD GETS IN YOUR WAY

READING: HAGGAI 1-2.

FOCUS: *Now then, consider from this day onward. Before stone was placed upon stone in the temple of the LORD, how did you fare? When one came to a heap of twenty measures, there were but ten. When one came to the wine vat to draw fifty measures, there were but twenty. I struck you and all the products of your toil with blight and with mildew and with hail, yet you did not turn to me, declares the LORD. Consider from this day onward, from the twenty-fourth day of the ninth month. Since the day that the foundation of the LORD's temple was laid, consider: Is the seed yet in the barn? Indeed, the vine, the fig tree, the pomegranate, and the olive tree have yielded nothing. But from this day on I will bless you.*

Haggai 2:15-19

Sometimes living in a fallen world is frustrating. Okay, *many* times living in a fallen world is frustrating. We see the evidence all the time that the creation truly has been subjected to futility. (Romans 8:20) If only there were a vaccine for futility! But things not going as we would want them to go is never simply a random event that just sort of "happens." When we trust in God's sovereignty in our lives, we know that nothing is truly random or accidental. God did not pat us on the head, wish us well and then leave us to chance when He created us to live in His world. He is present and He is involved.

Many years ago, the prophet Haggai spoke to a group of people who also were experiencing the futility and frustration of life on this planet. (At least, we can be comforted in knowing we're not the only ones!) They were putting in the time and effort but were not prospering. In fact, despite all they were doing, things were getting increasingly worse. Imagine checking your bank account; and without spending any money, your balance continues to decrease. That was very much like their experience.

The frustration would have been at an all-time high; but these people who had returned to Jerusalem, after the Exile, were painfully slow to understand what was happening to them. All that they had labored to possess and enjoy was being devoured; and for a time, they simply could not understand why. The opposition came from the Lord, but they were not catching on. The Lord was causing their plans to fail and their lives to be filled with emptiness — at least for a season.

Understand that God was not against them, and what was happening to them was not the wrath of God but rather His correction and discipline. The futility they continued to encounter was for their good. They were His people; and to some degree, they were doing His work; and God was persistent in trying to get their attention. Like some other people you may know, however, these people were dense. They had a difficult time taking the hint. Often the issue is not that God isn't speaking, but we are focused on more pressing matters – *ourselves.*

In their case, they had given priority to building their own houses, while the Temple of the Lord still lay in ruins. More than a building project, God knew that He did not really have their hearts and was not their highest priority.

The similarities between the people of Haggai's day and our lives are striking and convicting, but one notable difference is they didn't have the record of their example as we do. We're not necessarily building a Temple, but we do find multiple ways to place our priorities and agendas ahead of the things we know God wants us to be doing. What we are slow to understand is that our effectiveness in anything is limited when God isn't blessing our efforts. When Jesus said that apart from Him, we can do nothing (John 15:5), He wasn't suggesting that we couldn't still be awfully busy — even as we accomplish next to nothing.

Part of the futility we experience is simply the inevitable result of living in a fallen world, but could there be other ways in which God is trying to get our attention? We really don't want to find ourselves opposed by God because that's the only way that He can get our attention and get us to consider His plans and purposes. Maybe we're pursuing the wrong things, or maybe we're pursuing the right things but for the wrong reasons.

The encouraging thing about the book of Haggai is that the people finally clued in and changed their ways. When they did, God was ready to help instead of hinder. "But from this day on I will bless you." No words could have been more welcome. Of course, getting on board with God's plans and purposes does not remove us from a fallen world; but there are blessings we will enjoy only on the path of obedience when God occupies the place of highest priority in our lives. Even as so many things battle for our attention and our affection, may we give ourselves continually to His purposes over and above our own.

HEAD TO HEART

- In what specific ways have you been frustrated by the futility of life in a broken world?

- When you experience futility and frustration, what is your typical "go-to" response? Do you blame others, blame yourself or blame God?

- How do you seek to ensure that the priorities of your life are aligned with His? What do you do when they clearly are not?

DAY 38

ZECHARIAH: HIS PART, OUR PART
READING: ZECHARIAH 4.

FOCUS: *Then he said to me, "This is the word of the LORD to Zerubbabel: Not by might, nor by power, but by my Spirit, says the LORD of hosts. Who are you, O great mountain? Before Zerubbabel you shall become a plain. And he shall bring forward the top stone amid shouts of 'Grace, grace to it!'" Then the word of the LORD came to me, saying, "The hands of Zerubbabel have laid the foundation of this house; his hands shall also complete it. Then you will know that the LORD of hosts has sent me to you. For whoever has despised the day of small things shall rejoice, and shall see the plumb line in the hand of Zerubbabel. These seven are the eyes of the LORD, which range through the whole earth."*

Zechariah 4:6-10

You may remember the classic story *Where the Red Fern Grows* by Wilson Rawls about a young boy named Billy with two redbone hound dogs, Little Ann and Old Dan. As the story unfolds, the long-awaited moment when the dogs treed their first coon finally had arrived. The problem was that the wily, old coon ran up into the largest tree in the whole forest. For the sake of his dogs and his own sake as well, not felling the tree and leaving the coon behind simply were not options. So Billy took his ax and began to hack away at the huge tree. After two full days of chopping, Billy had blistered hands and aching muscles that made it impossible for him to continue. The dogs, knowing the coon was still in the tree, whimpered and whined as Billy sobbed in agony. He had done all he could do, and all he could do was still not enough.

And then Billy prayed. He knew he needed help and asked for the strength to keep chopping. With all of his strength gone and yet wrapping his hands so he could continue, Billy suddenly noticed a breeze in the top of the huge tree. He also noticed that all of the surrounding trees remained still. Then another gust came, and slowly the big sycamore tree began to crack and moan in the wind and finally crashed to the ground with a roar. Billy had done all he could do, but only God could have sent the wind.

Could God have toppled the tree without Billy chopping? Of course. Could Billy have chopped the tree down on his own? No way. But he still did his part, then the wind blew and God got the glory. No one else was there to see what happened, but Billy knew he had been helped that day.

Nice story, but what does that have to do with Zechariah? A part of the reason for Zechariah's writing was that Zerubbabel, one of the leaders of the restoration of Jerusalem, needed to be encouraged that all of his labor hadn't been in vain. In a similar way, Zerubbabel could not do all the work on his own, but he had labored diligently to do what he could. Now God was going to ensure that the work was completed. God allowed Zerubbabel to lay the foundation of the restored Temple, and He would ensure that the work would be completed. The many days and many efforts of preparation were not wasted.

Zechariah refers to such days as the "day of small things." Zerubbabel knew them well just as many of us also have experienced days that we considered to be small and insignificant. We simply chop away with no end or victory in sight. But those days and those seasons are not wasted because, even more than we are, God is committed to finishing the work that He has started in us. All that has happened in your life to bring you to this point has not been wasted but ordained in preparation for the fulfillment of His purpose. Where He has appointed you to labor to lay the foundation, He also will complete the work so that you will see and know that He did the part that only He could do.

One of the most difficult things for us to overcome in our spiritual journey is our determination to do things our way and in our strength. While that strategy never once has been effective ultimately we still tend to fall back into old patterns. The word of the Lord through Zechariah was: "Not by might, nor by power, but by my Spirit." Nothing we do will succeed apart from God granting the increase, but our part really does matter. The prophet Haggai had a similar encouragement: "Yet now be strong, O Zerubbabel, declares the LORD. Be strong, O Joshua, son of Jehozadak, the high priest. Be strong, all you people of the land, declares the LORD. *Work, for I am with you,* declares the LORD of hosts" (emphasis mine, Haggai 2:4).

We can rest in knowing that the work isn't all up to us and rejoice in knowing that God has chosen to use each of us to fulfill His purposes. God could work without us but allows us to be a part. Many years later, Paul also would explain this dynamic. "Therefore, my beloved, as you have always obeyed, so now, not only as in my presence but much more in my absence, work out your own salvation with fear and trembling, for it is God who works in you, both to will and to work for his good pleasure" (Philippians 2:12–13). We "work out" because He works in us. Chop away – do your part, do the work – and watch what happens when the wind starts to blow.

HEAD TO HEART

- Do you fall off on the side of trying to do things in your strength, or on the side of not doing anything if your efforts might be wasted?

- What are some specific times in which you know you were helped and strengthened by God?

- How have you seen God use you for His purposes when He easily could have done the work without you?

DAY 39

MALACHI: HOW HAVE YOU LOVED US?

READING: MALACHI 1.

FOCUS: *The oracle of the word of the LORD to Israel by Malachi. "I have loved you," says the LORD. But you say, "How have you loved us?" "Is not Esau Jacob's brother?" declares the LORD. "Yet I have loved Jacob but Esau I have hated. I have laid waste his hill country and left his heritage to jackals of the desert." If Edom says, "We are shattered but we will rebuild the ruins," the LORD of hosts says, "They may build, but I will tear down, and they will be called 'the wicked country,' and 'the people with whom the LORD is angry forever.'" Your own eyes shall see this, and you shall say, "Great is the LORD beyond the border of Israel!" "A son honors his father, and a servant his master. If then I am a father, where is my honor? And if I am a master, where is my fear? says the LORD of hosts to you, O priests, who despise my name. But you say, 'How have we despised your name?'*

Malachi 1:1-6

Had the people of Israel fully understood what was about to happen at the conclusion of Yahweh's words through the prophet Malachi, they might have listened more carefully. Then again, probably not. They were disregarding what He had said already, so there is little reason to believe anything would have changed. But at the conclusion of Malachi, God ceased speaking to His people *for the next 400 years.*

Now God was known to refrain from speaking on occasion. He remained silent as Job agonized in 37 chapters of misery and frustration. Habakkuk asked why God remained silent while evil was seemingly winning the day. (Habakkuk 1:13) Clearly, David had experienced the silence of Heaven as he frequently asked God to not be silent or distant. (Psalm 35:22) In each situation, however, God finally spoke; and when He did, He spoke decisively.

But 400 years of silence is a long time. On this side of Jesus' life, death and resurrection, we have the benefit of the rest of the story to see that God was preparing the way and setting the stage for the Word. (John 1:1) The Word (Jesus) not only would speak to us but would become one of us, but He came only after God had been silent for so long.

Obviously, the Lord was not taken by surprise by the actions or attitudes of His people; but what prompted His silence in response? And is it possible that we aren't hearing the voice of the Holy Spirit in our lives today for some of the same reasons? Sometimes we don't hear His voice because He simply isn't ready to speak, and so we wait. But other times, our disobedience and self-absorption entail that He is waiting for us to turn to Him in repentance. In other words, He is waiting to speak until we are ready to listen.

When God spoke of His love for His people through Malachi, their response was to ask, "How have You loved us?" How? Their question may as well have been: "But what have You done for us *lately*?" Their response to God's love was brazen arrogance and entitlement. They were spoiled and unaffected by the love and favor God continually had shown them already.

For example, the Lord reminded them that He had chosen their ancestor Jacob and rejected his twin brother Esau, who was the ancestor of the Edomites. (Genesis 25; Romans 9:13) When God allowed the Edomites and their land to be destroyed, He said that He would not let them rebuild — even if they tried. In contrast, the people of Judah in Malachi's day were living proof that God had brought restoration even after He had allowed His people to be carried away into Exile. In God's mercy, a remnant had returned, and the rebuilding had been underway for many years at this point. The very fact that they were alive and in Judah demonstrated that God had shown them great favor and mercy.

Ingratitude and a painfully short-sighted view of God's providence had plagued His chosen people from the time the Lord miraculously had brought them out of Egypt up until the present. They did not look to the future in the light of how God had been so faithful in the past. They did not see in the present the many ways in which God had blessed and provided for them. When we recognize these attitudes and understand how long God endured that kind of thing from His people, we know that God wasn't being petty or temperamental in the four-century "silent treatment" that would begin soon. Thankfully, God broke the silence when He sent His Son.

Part of the reason the Holy Spirit moved people to write and preserve the words of the Old Testament is so that we might have a mirror to hold up to our lives. Many of the pictures we see of God's people in those days are ugly and painful, but those same tendencies are ever present in our lives. We struggle with ungrateful hearts when God does not answer a prayer according to our wishes. Sometimes we don't get the answer we wanted and don't understand why, but only a shallow faith requires God to jump through hoops and doubts God's goodness every time a prayer isn't answered in the way that we see fit.

We wholeheartedly assume that the lives of others are so much better than our own and thus conclude that God is holding out on us. Our assumption can be there are innumerable blessings that others have and we should have them all, too. But is God's goodness not powerfully seen in refusing us the things that would be hurtful? We often doubt God's goodness because of His "no" when His "no" is a demonstration of His grace. His mercy is displayed when He does not simply say to us, "Fine! Have it *your* way."

More than likely, you are reading devotions from the Old Testament because you genuinely want to know the presence of the Lord in your life and live in a way that glorifies God. Malachi and his contemporaries only could look forward in hope, and they clearly struggled in their faith as they did. But unlike them, we don't have to hope that God will do something, that God will help us, that God will bless us.

Stop. Breathe. And remember the Cross. Even if in the current moment, God seems to be doing nothing, *remember it is finished.* Romans 8:32 says, "He who did not spare his own Son but gave him up for us all, how will he not also with him graciously give us all things?" Keep praying. Keep trusting. Keep believing. But as you do, remember that what He has already done is more than enough.

HEAD TO HEART

- Do you struggle when God does not seem to be meeting your perceived needs?

- Do you think ingratitude is more a matter of neglect or of deliberate choices? In other words, what is the "why" behind an ungrateful heart?

- In what specific ways can you practice gratitude to God in your everyday life?

DAY 40

LOOKING BACK: THAT WE MIGHT HAVE HOPE

READING: ROMANS 15:1-13.

FOCUS: *For whatever was written in former days was written for our instruction, that through endurance and through the encouragement of the Scriptures we might have hope. May the God of endurance and encouragement grant you to live in such harmony with one another, in accord with Christ Jesus, that together you may with one voice glorify the God and Father of our Lord Jesus Christ.*

Romans 15:4-6

God gave us a gift, and that gift is one that truly keeps on giving. The gift we call the Old Testament continues to be opened when we make the effort to unwrap and unpack its wisdom and instruction. When Paul wrote to the Christians in Rome and referenced the Scriptures, he primarily meant the Old Testament since the New Testament was still in the process of being written and compiled. Although Jesus fulfilled the Law and was the final sacrifice for our sins, Paul wanted Christians to understand that the Scriptures still were useful — although many of the specific laws now were obsolete.

Through all of the tedious laws, the inglorious history, the puzzling poetry and the exasperated prophets, God gave us His instruction in the Old Testament. We learn from their victories and perhaps even more from their failures. No further case needs to be made that people truly need a Savior. But even in the repetitious futility, we see God's sovereign hand – on some occasions working behind the scenes but at other times powerfully asserting His authority.

Abraham, Moses and many others put their faith and trust in God and looked forward to the Cross when He, once and for all, would redeem

His people. We live as many years after Jesus' sacrifice as some of them lived before those pivotal events, but we look to the same Savior Whom God sent in the fullness of time. God had a plan for them and for us, and His glorious plan is coming together even now. The writer of Hebrews connects the faithful of old to those who have saving faith today. "And all these, though commended through their faith, did not receive what was promised, since God had provided something better for us, that apart from us they should not be made perfect" (Hebrews 11:39–40).

We are part of God's plan that has been in place from the beginning. Many have gone before us — the ones who trusted God in the Old Testament and all those since then who have been saved by grace through faith. Hebrews continues: "Therefore, since we are surrounded by so great a cloud of witnesses, let us also lay aside every weight, and sin which clings so closely, and let us run with endurance the race that is set before us, looking to Jesus, the founder and perfecter of our faith, who for the joy that was set before him endured the cross, despising the shame, and is seated at the right hand of the throne of God" (Hebrews 12:1–2).

Paul wrote to a group of Christians in Rome who were enduring trials and difficulties. The Holy Spirit moved Paul to encourage and exhort them towards unity and away from selfishness. In the midst of struggles, we tend to focus only on ourselves; but God gave us the Scriptures to help us endure and to encourage us as well. The word used for endurance literally means "to remain or stand under" — the idea that we bear the weight of the trial. Of course, we need His help to do this; but that is where His Word encourages us as we do. We're reminded that endurance is necessary because the journey is hard. We're encouraged because God remained faithful to them — just as He will carry us all the way to the end of our journey.

As we endure and continually receive the encouragement of His Word, the end result is that we have hope. The hope that He gives is not some vague, generally optimistic or even naïve approach to life in this world. The hope that we have in Jesus is based on the assurance that God is Who He says He is and will do what He says He will do.

Earlier in Romans, Paul writes: "Therefore, since we have been justified by faith, we have peace with God through our Lord Jesus Christ. Through him we have also obtained access by faith into this grace in which we stand, and we rejoice in hope of the glory of God. Not only that, but we rejoice in our sufferings, knowing that suffering produces endurance, and endurance produces character, and character produces hope, and hope does not put us to shame, because God's love has been poured into our hearts through the Holy Spirit who has been given to us" (Romans 5:1–5). As we keep on trusting and keep on enduring, we will not be disappointed or put to shame because our hope has been grounded in Him.

May the Lord continue to bless your life. May you continue to love, study and obey His Word as you run the race that He has set before you. And finally, "May the God of hope fill you with all joy and peace in believing, so that by the power of the Holy Spirit you may abound in hope" (Romans 15:13).

HEAD TO HEART

- How does the Old Testament help us to understand the New Testament?

- How have Old Testament passages encouraged and emboldened you in your journey?

- In all the sorrows and struggles of this life, are you abounding in hope?

ALSO FROM THE OLD TESTAMENT DEVOTIONAL SERIES

ANCIENT PATHS:
Light and Life from the Scriptures Jesus Read

FEET OF CLAY:
Failures from Yesterday, New Mercies for Today

Available on Amazon and other retailers
or directly from the author:

www.mountaintime.org
orders@mountaintime.org

www.ingramcontent.com/pod-product-compliance
Lightning Source LLC
Chambersburg PA
CBHW060802050426
42449CB00008B/1501